K

H

Across the Top of the World

Across the Top of the World

The British Trans-Arctic Expedition

Wally Herbert

Longmans

Longman Group Ltd
London and Harlow

*Associated companies, branches and representatives
throughout the world*

© *The British Trans-Arctic Expedition* 1969

First published 1969

SBN 582 10801 2

*Printed in Great Britain by
T. and A. Constable Ltd, Edinburgh*

This book is dedicated to my companions of the Expedition, and to the Expedition's Committee without whose vision, confidence and encouragement, the first surface crossing of the Arctic Ocean could not have been accomplished.

Squadron Leader Freddie Church, RAF
Allan Gill
Major Ken Hedges, MB, CH.B., RAMC
Dr Roy Koerner

Sir Miles Clifford, KBE, CMG, ED, HON.FRCS (Chairman)
Colonel Andrew Croft, DSO
Sir Vivian Fuchs, MA, PH.D.
The Rt. Hon. Lord Hunt, CBE, DSO
Rear-Admiral Sir Edmund Irving, KBE, CB
Mr G. P. Pirie-Gordon (Hon. Treasurer)
H.E. Sir Arthur Porritt, Bt., GCMG, KCVO, CBE, FRCS
   (Governor General of New Zealand)
Mr A. G. Tritton (Hon. Secretary)

Contents

List of Illustrations

List of Illustrations—*contd.*

Prologue

A BLUE–GREY FOG WAS TUMBLING SOFTLY ROUND A DEAD CAMP-FIRE WHEN I AWOKE COLD AND STIFF ON THE morning of 18 June 1960, rolled out of a depression in the spongy tundra, launched a kayak and resumed my journey along the fjord. In the past three days I had paddled eighty miles through breaking seas, along a coastline aproned in scree and scarred by rushing melt streams; under towering, fluted cliffs and curtains of nesting birds, and through the ice-choked waters in front of the Von Post and Tuna glaciers. It was a race against time – a race to catch the S.S. *Lyngen* which was due to sail south on the morning of the 19th June from the mining town of Longyearbyen, the largest township on the Arctic island of Spitzbergen.

My stay on the island had been a short one. I had, during the past four weeks, been a member of an expedition, the object of which had been to carry out physiological experiments to see if the human being could adapt to an abnormal length of day. It had been a pleasant and relaxing period for my companions, Dr Hugh Simpson, Myrtle his wife, Fred Bruemmer and myself, and our routine of research was simple. There had been no isolation, no great stress or hardship, no time for discontent to mar our relationships. For a month we had lazily watched the urgency of life around us as birds flew to and fro all day, or sat and strained to lay their eggs while the sun baked their backs and the tundra steamed around them. We had watched the eggs hatch out and heard a symphony of bird song rise in pitch and volume. Snow bed plants had burst into bloom. Melt pools

I

that had teamed with larvae became dance floors of gnats, black midges and mosquitoes. Warmth drew the vegetable matter, and the odour had set the insects humming. Warmth had melted the surface of the glaciers; water, perspiring down the smooth green creases, trickled in streams which joined up and became torrents, boiling and cascading with a roar into crevasses which filled up and overflowed. Huge blocks of overhanging ice, eaten loose by the flow of melt water and the ambient pressures in the glacier, had broken and crashed into Tempelfjord – the fjord in which, without then knowing it, I would one day plan to end a trans-polar journey of 3,800 miles.

Fog muted everything that morning; even the plunging kayak made only a dull thud as I hugged the cliffs which rose sheer from a thin line of froth. Many times during that day they drifted away into the mist and by evening, as I drew in to the coast alongside a cluster of derelict shacks on the opposite side of a small tributary fjord from my destination, I was fatigued and frozen to the core. It was two miles from there across to Longyearbyen, but I had no reserves of energy to cover that short distance in order to stay the night in that mining town where gently swaying aerial coal tubs, like wingless buzzards, moved silently in slow procession above barrack blocks and sheds from which men occasionally emerged and scampered quickly out of sight as though afraid of daylight. I had, in any case, on my first visit to Longyearbyen been far too depressed by the scene of dereliction and its covering of dust to feel any inclination to spend another night in that god-forsaken spot, and so had elected to doss down in some sheltered nook amongst the deserted mine-workings of Moskushamn.

A wiry, strained-faced man appeared, strode down to the water's edge, greeted me in English and lifted the kayak high above the beach. We picked our way through the debris of broken-down buildings, rusted engines and abandoned mine-workings towards a warped three-storeyed warehouse. Most of its windows were shuttered and the groaning door flapped gently on its hinges. Inside the warehouse it was dark. Pit props supported a sagging ceiling. The whole building seemed to be listing, and the rotting staircase creaked as we climbed to the attic.

My host was the only inhabitant of Moskushamn, a recluse who had spent two previous winters on the north coast of Spitzbergen hunting polar bear. He was at that time gathering together stores and equipment for another winter, and the squalid attic was his temporary retreat until the autumn when he would be shipped by sealing vessel up the coast, occupy his tiny hut, bait his traps, set his fixed guns and wait for the bear to come. He was a man with a stare in his eyes; a man who wintered alone by choice – a nocturnal man who awakens at sundown and prowls around in polar darkness.

It was several hours before I felt at ease in his company, for surprisingly he was intense; a nervous man, a man of great intelligence – enigmatic and yet in some ways very simple. Not for him the expedition with its snug comforts and scientific programmes. He was an aesthete, a poet, a hunter. We came from different worlds, he and I, and yet we spoke a common language, and while the wind moaned past the windows, we talked away the hours of sleep.

We talked about the life he led and about his techniques of hunting. We talked about the polar bear and about the polar basin.

'Why is it,' he asked, 'that no one has ever attempted to sledge across the Arctic Ocean?'

'Because it is not feasible,' I told him, without giving it much thought.

1 Polar Background

Polar exploration, like most other fields of human endeavour, has seen a variety of motives, but since the urge to explore the polar regions held less commercial attractions than most other parts of the world, the motives in general were purer and man found there, as he is now finding in space, a nobler outlet for his curiosity, his patriotism and his love of adventure, that attribute of a higher civilization which calls for excursions into new environments and new experiences 'for its own sake'. Examples that come to mind are the numerous attempts which resulted in the conquest of Mount Everest by a British expedition in 1953 and the first surface crossing of the Antarctic Continent by the Commonwealth Trans-Antarctic Expedition in 1958.

In 1913, the motives of Sir Ernest Shackleton in proposing the first crossing of the Antarctic had been basically the same – he had argued that a trans-Antarctic journey was the last great journey that could be made, for neither the South Pole nor the North Pole were any longer legitimate goals, both having been reached by sledging parties. As for the crossing of the Arctic Ocean, it was then, by all but one man (Alfred H. Harrison), considered impossible.

Shackleton's proposal for an imperial trans-Antarctic expedition was a natural next step in polar exploration which at the same time gave hope of action for his restless spirit and vent to a nation's patriotism. Speaking at a meeting of the Royal Geographical Society in February 1914 he stated that '. . . first and foremost, the main object of the expedition is the crossing

5

of the Polar Continent from sea to sea. Some people condemn this object as being spectacular and of no particular use and consider that no expedition should set forth without the one object of being purely scientific. Until the South Pole had been reached, deep in the minds of every explorer who penetrated the Antarctic, was the desire to reach this goal. My desire is to cross the Antarctic Continent and in undertaking this expedition, the members of it are agents of the British Nation. If I said differently, I would be untrue to my convictions. I have put the crossing of the Continent as the great object in this expedition and there is not one person in this room tonight, and there is not one individual under the Union Jack in any part of the Empire, who does not wish the British flag to be the first national flag ever carried across the frozen wastes.'

He went on to outline his plan for research but drew his narration to a close by insisting that primarily his expedition was 'a sporting feat' – a phrase which, not surprisingly, alarmed the officers of the Royal Geographical Society, who considered themselves, to use Shackleton's words: '. . . the keepers of the conscience of the geographical world'. Nevertheless, his expedition was supported by that Society, for any expedition which is a pioneer journey is, by its very nature, an exploration. By the same argument, the first surface crossing of the Arctic Ocean was an exploration and, in its historical setting, the culmination of three hundred and sixty years of polar endeavour; for with the advent of aircraft and submarines, man had left unfulfilled his ambition physically to master the polar environment and had left uncompleted a journey across the top of the world – a journey which was attempted for the first time in recorded history by an Englishman, Henry Hudson, in 1607.

During the early fifteenth century, under the rival flags of Portugal and Spain, voyage after voyage had been made in search of a sea route to the Orient, for news of the immense wealth of Cathay brought back by Marco Polo's desert caravans had dazzled the European world and by 1540, with the Portuguese in command of the sea route around Africa, and the Spanish in command of the route around South America, little choice was left for the younger maritime nations of Europe but to penetrate the north in search of trade routes to the riches of the East.

Of all the northern lands discovered by the Vikings in the tenth century and occupied by Colonies during the three centuries that followed, Iceland alone had remained part of the known world, for the Norsemen had died and carried with them to their graves their knowledge of the Arctic. But Viking blood, with its heritage of courage and its tradition of restless seafaring, had helped to create England, and five centuries after the Vikings had discovered their Arctic world, the English had taken to the sea.

The seafaring skills that were to become the pride of a nation, however, had not been acquired entirely by instinct. The Englishman's knowledge of geography had come from abroad, so had his system of navigation; but the skills were soon taken into the blood, and when young Edward VI had come to the throne, one of the first things he had done was to induce Sebastian Cabot (the chief navigator of Spain) to become the grand pilot of England and to coach the precocious mariners for a greater destiny. England was moving rapidly into a new age of expansion. Sebastian Cabot was made 'Governour of the mysterie and companie of the merchants adventurers for the discoverie of regions, dominions, islands and places unknowen', and immediately the company had set about planning a voyage of discovery, north-west to the Orient.

But in this first period of polar exploration, men were in such fear of the north that even the boldest of them dared only brief summer excursions into the ice-strewn seas. Polar darkness was dreaded like the torments of hell, and those forced to spend the winter in the Arctic had found that it was 'dark, dark, dark ... without all hope of day' and died miserably of scurvy. Their diaries told of suffering and hopeless courage; of storms, disease

7

and intense cold. The Elizabethans, however, were not easily put off; their Queen approved of the search of trade routes to the Orient which promised wealth for her kingdom and the command of the northern seas, and with the exception of the temporary distraction of fighting off the Spanish Armada, the Elizabethan polar explorers – notably Frobisher, Davis and Hudson – became almost obsessed with their search for the illusive passage to the East.

It was the age of discovery. Discovery was the key that opened the doors of trade. It was the age of undreamed-of wealth. It was the age that gave birth to the great trading companies whose profits were used to promote further exploration. The company of merchants adventurers, as a result of their first polar expedition of 1553, had founded the Muscovy Company which developed a very lucrative trade exchange between England and Russia via the northern sea route. From profits of this Company, Henry Hudson's voyages of discovery were financed – an investment in exploration which paid dividends in plenty, for at Hudson's reports that the Spitzbergen waters were seething with whales there developed a piratical battle for oil. Fleets of whaling ships from every maritime nation, in direct competition with each other, despoiled and exterminated the great sea mammals in a gory rush of slaughter; and when the whaling was exhausted, a new territory was tapped and a new enterprise formed – the Hudson's Bay Company – which gathered in millions of pounds from the animal skins of Northern Canada, and always, as security, there were the fishing harvests off the banks of Newfoundland. Was it any wonder that the north had such a hold upon the imagination of the English – the nation that fed and grew upon its bounty?

For three and a half centuries, from the reign of King Henry VIII until 1882 (with the exception of the twelve years between 1594 and 1606, when through Willem Barents, the Dutch held the record), the flag of Great Britain flew nearest the top of the world. John Davis reached latitude 72° 41' N on the west coast

8

of Greenland in 1587. Henry Hudson advanced the record to 80°23′ N in 1607 while searching for a way through the pack ice of the Greenland sea towards what was supposedly an open polar ocean and a direct route over the Pole to the East.

Hudson's record remained unequalled for one hundred and sixty-five years, until 1773, when Captain the Honourable Constantine Phipps surpassed his farthest north by twenty-five miles in Spitzbergen waters with a well-appointed naval scientific expedition which was attempting to reach the North Pole directly by sea. The expedition is memorable, however, not for its record northing, or for its extraordinarily bad survey of Spitzbergen, but because one of the midshipmen was Horatio Nelson – a mischievous lad of fourteen whose destiny it was to lead his country to many a naval victory.

The re-awakening of polar exploration after the Napoleonic Wars was freshly motivated. Popular enthusiasms, broadly speaking, were becoming more scientific; while the Navy – mistress of the seas since the Battle of Trafalgar – was eager to test her men and ships against a sterner foe. It was now no longer the North-West Passage to Cathay they were seeking; it was the exploration and extension of British Arctic Territory. As an added incentive to explorers, an Act of Parliament was passed in 1818 (similar to one of 1776) offering a reward of £20,000 for the discovery of the North-West Passage and £5,000 for the attainment of the North Pole.

Officers and men of the Royal Navy volunteered for Arctic service and, dressed in uniforms more appropriate to Portsmouth than the polar regions, drove their ships against the ice which blocked their route to the Pole or through the intricate channels of the Canadian Archipelago. Of such stern stuff were these sailors made. They considered it their privilege to suffer. Instead of fleeing south with the setting sun as the Elizabethan mariners had done, the Royal Navy hibernated beneath a canopy of canvas covering the decks of their ships – their winter quarters until spring.

Outstanding among the many famous polar explorers of the early nineteenth century was Edward Parry. He was given his first command of a polar expedition at the age of twenty-nine; but already his achievements were considerable. He had been John Ross's second-in-command in 1818 when an abortive attempt had been made on the North-West Passage. He was a Fellow of the Royal Society, a masterly navigator with a genius for leadership. His expedition, which sailed in 1819 in the *Hecla* and *Griper*, was provisioned for three years, and his objective – the North-West Passage. Parry on that voyage penetrated deeper into the maze of channels than anyone before him, and in its record of good health and high morale, this first wintering of naval ships in the Arctic was a remarkable success. He was lionized in England and given the command of two other naval expeditions in search of the North-West Passage; expeditions that, although not as impressive as the first, were rich enough in experience for Parry to reach conclusions that were to revolutionize polar travel technique.

All previous attempts to reach the North Pole had been ship-borne, for it was believed that once through the belt of pack ice at the perimeter of the Arctic Ocean there would be open water beyond. Parry did not wholly accept this theory of the open Polar Sea, and 'proposed to attempt to reach the North Pole, by means of travelling with sledge boats over the ice, or through any spaces of water that might occur'. With a ship to transport him to a base on the edge of the Arctic Ocean, and an advance from his ship over the ice on foot, Parry inaugurated a technique that was to become common procedure for almost all later attempts at the Pole.

In his ship, the *Hecla*, he reached Treurenberg Bay on the north coast of Spitzbergen in early June 1827. From there, with twenty-seven men, provisioned for seventy-one days, they set out to reach the North Pole dragging boats shod with steel runners. They suffered inexpressible hardships, advancing blindly through fogs, rain and slush, over hummock ice and pressure, and along leads of open water. They toiled throughout the hours of evening, then took an hour off for dinner and resumed their labour until 'dawn'. Hauling their boats up on to a safe floe, they would spread the sails for a canopy, congregate for prayers, then suffer the hours of inaction until the bugle called them to another night of toil. They cheered to keep their spirits up, and set an example in heroism. As if on a treadmill they had travelled almost a thousand miles, although they had never actually been further than 172 miles from their ship. But Parry had set a record at 82°45' N which was unbeaten for half a century, and in originality of plan his attempt at the Pole has been unequalled by any Arctic explorer with the exception of Fridtjof Nansen.

The advancement of polar technique took a further step forward a few years later. Though far less dramatic than Parry's attempt at the North Pole, the voyage of the *Victory* (1829-34) in search of the North-West Passage brought Europeans for the first time into close association with the Eskimos and their technique of travel. This expedition, under the command of Captain John Ross, had both the distinction of discovering the North Magnetic Pole and of spending four consecutive winters in the Arctic without loss of life; and the break during the 1830s when the Royal Navy turned from Arctic to Antarctic exploration can very largely be attributed to Commander James Clark Ross (nephew of John Ross) who had been the specialist in magnetism aboard the *Victory*.

The Antarctic discoveries of James Clark Ross were the greatest geographical discoveries of the age. Laurels were heaped upon him by every nation, and no sooner had he returned to England than he was invited by the Admiralty to command a splendid 'final' assault on the North-West Passage, but Sir James Clark Ross (as he had now become) graciously declined the command, under pressure from his wife, and it was given instead to Sir John Franklin – a polar man of fifty-nine years of age, whose Arctic exploits were already legendary.

No expedition in the history of Arctic exploration had set out with a bolder anticipation of success than that of Franklin in 1845. His two ships, the *Erebus* and *Terra*, just refitted after their outstanding performance in the Antarctic with Ross, were the pride of the naval dockyards and were lavishly equipped. The hundred and thirty-four men were the pick of the Royal Navy, and Franklin the idol of the nation. But they sailed into a mystery that took a decade to solve, a mystery which involved some forty ships and more than two thousand men before the picture of distress, disease and cannibalism was put together piece by piece.

The tragedy and subsequent search for Franklin's expedition, however, accelerated the discovery and exploration of the Canadian Archipelago, solved the long-drawn-out question of the North-West Passage and introduced new men, new techniques and new motives to the North. By the end of the decade explorers had abandoned the worn-out methods of the past – the ship-borne expeditions with their silver plate, hand organs and blue serge Navy suits – and through the pioneering example of Leopold McClintock had taken to the Eskimo methods of travel. With the surge of freedom this change brought to polar exploration, it was but a short stride from there to the Pole.

In the motives for going north there developed an analogy to mountaineering. The North Pole was seen as a prize; the summit of a super-mountain; the top of the world. It attracted men who were hard travellers and exciting story-tellers. On generous public subscriptions, payments for exclusive rights of publications and various other means of raising money, the adventurer explorers had set out. Dr Eliza Kent Kane, an American, was the first of these Arctic 'characters' to enter the field.

America had taken no active part in Arctic explorations until the Franklin search had aroused their sympathy, and Kane, playing on this sympathy, had no difficulty in raising money for an expedition which combined a search for Franklin with an attempt to reach the North Pole via the Sound separating Greenland from Ellesmere Island – a route which became known as the American route to the Pole. In spite of inexperience which resulted in scurvy, fatal accidents and the loss of a ship, Kane's achievement in 1853-55 won him widespread acclaim, and he was soon followed by another American, Dr Isaac Israel Hayes. Both of them believed in the theory of 'the open polar sea', although it was left to another American, Charles Francis Hall, to be the first man to reach the edge of the Arctic Ocean.

Hall was an impoverished printer, with apparently little to qualify him as a potential polar explorer. His forays into the Arctic were often one-man affairs; but by living with Eskimos and adapting himself to the native techniques, he came nearer than any explorer before him to making a successful assault on the Pole. In a tug commissioned by the U.S. Navy Department and renamed the *Polaris*, Hall sailed in 1871 up the channels leading from Baffin Bay to the Arctic Ocean, and reached the unequalled northing for those waters of 82°11' N. But the strain of his efforts over the years took its toll. Hall died, the *Polaris* was struck by a floe, and as the party were in the process of abandoning the reeling ship, it was blown away, leaving behind on the ice nineteen of the ship's company, including two families of Eskimos, some scant provisions, two kayaks, two whale-boats and a compass. They drifted southwards through the winter on their ever-diminishing ice floe for one thousand three hundred miles before they were rescued in a pitiful state of starvation off the coast of Labrador in 1874. That was the year of the birth of Ernest Henry Shackleton, who as a boy was enthralled by the account of the *Polaris* expedition – as indeed was a vast reading public, who found in the blend of heroism, folk-lore and sporting challenge a growing excitement in the drama of the attainment of the Pole.

The *Polaris* expedition and the gathering interest of the

Americans in the challenge of the Pole goaded the Royal Navy into a determined effort to claim the Pole for Britain, and in 1875, two fine ships, the *Alert* and the *Discovery*, under the command of Captain George Nares, sailed for the route so recently extended by Hall to the edge of the Polar Sea. But although Nares as a lieutenant had had the benefit of service with McClintock, his 1875-76 expedition was a relapse into the complacent spirit of the late Victorian Navy.

That the expedition succeeded in surpassing all northern records hitherto made was in no way due to the method, but rather to the superb skill with which Nares navigated his two ships to the very edge of the Arctic Ocean, and to the grit of his officers and men who, like Parry's men of half a century earlier, dragged their ponderous boats northwards, and, by sheer patriotic fervour, planted the Union Jack north of the previous record. But the smell of tragedy had hung over that expedition from the start, and the toll of scurvy was devastating – fifty-six men out of a complement of one hundred and twenty-one – and yet those men rose to new heights of heroism and survived.

Attempts at the Pole were numerous in the years that lay ahead, but the English lost their interest in the North Pole and in 1882 they also lost their record farthest north to an American expedition led by Major Adolphus Greely. The Greely expedition, however, through the indecision and incompetence of the home administration and the relief operations, was reduced from twenty-five men to a starving huddle of seven survivors.

The suffering that marked this period in Arctic history was not confined to the vicinity of Northern Ellesmere Island, for preceding the epic drift of Nansen's *Fram* across the Arctic Ocean in 1893 to 1896, was the tragic voyage of the *Jeannette*. The leader of the expedition was Lieutenant George Washington De Long, an American sailor of exceptional courage, who was already hardened by Arctic experience. He had been strongly influenced by the theory of two young Austrian explorers, Karl Weyprect and Julius Payer, who believed that the islands of Franz Joseph Land (which they had discovered while attempting to reach the North Pole in 1871-73) were really outliers of a continental land mass – a proposition no stranger than the theory of the open polar sea, but one which revealed the ignorance which existed about the nature of the polar basin to as late as the nineteenth century. De Long planned to find this new land by sailing into the Arctic Ocean through the Bering Straits and taking advantage of the warm, north-flowing Japanese currents which he believed would open a way through the pack ice.

De Long sailed through the Bering Straits at the end of August 1879 and within a week the *Jeanette* was in the pack ice. Off Herald Island she was beset, and for the next seventeen months drifted in a north-westerly direction slowly, tortuously – the 'thirty-three men wearing out their lives and souls like men doomed to imprisonment for life'. On 12th June 1881, the *Jeannette* sank north-east of the New Siberian Islands, and hauling their three boats on sledges over the treacherous pack ice the crew of the *Jeannette* made their way towards the mainland at the head of the Lena River; but one cutter was lost in a gale with the lives of eight men, while of De Long's cutter, only two men out of the ten survived the tramp across the Lena Delta – De Long being among those who died of cold and hunger. Only the crew of the whale boat under the command of George Melville survived the ordeal, and one of them ended up in an asylum for the insane.

Three years after the *Jeannette* had sunk, debris and scraps of clothing that had littered the floe near the grave of the ship were found embedded in the ice that had been washed ashore in South-West Greenland. A Norwegian scholar, Fridtjof Nansen, then only twenty-three years of age, had read about this in a newspaper article by Professor Mohn in the autumn of 1884, and immediately realized that 'if a floe could drift right across the unknown regions, that drift might be enlisted in the service of exploration'. His daring plan was born: he would build a ship which would ride up on the ice as pressure squeezed the hull – a small stout vessel it had to be, with sail and auxiliary engines, a vessel provisioned for five years which would be driven into the ice in the vicinity of the New Siberian Islands and drift with the currents across the Arctic Ocean towards the Greenland Sea. Many problems of the Arctic Basin would be solved by such a voyage. It would settle once and for all whether there existed a continent or an open polar sea; the nature of the currents; the depth and temperature of the water; the nature of the drifting ice, and whether there was any animal life in the Arctic Ocean.

His plan was not put into immediate operation, and many years passed, years during which Nansen tested his mettle by making the first crossing of Greenland; but his theory of the polar drift was seldom far from his mind, and in November 1892 he travelled to London to lay his plans (as I myself was to do seventy-three years later) before the Royal Geographical Society. At that historic meeting, the simplicity and revolutionary daring of his plan alarmed practically all the polar pundits; but despite the condemnation of so many of its members, the Society, with an English illogicality, contributed £300 towards his expedition. On 24 June 1893, nine years after he had first read the article that had inspired the venture, his ship, the *Fram*, with thirteen men on board, set sail to put his theory to the test.

The *Fram* performed perfectly, rising above ice floes that would have crushed any other ship, and drifted, as Nansen had predicted, across the Polar Basin. But as time went on it became apparent that the *Fram* would not drift over the Pole but would by-pass it, and the adventurer in Nansen (getting the upper hand of the scientist in him) compelled him to set out with Lieutenant F. H. Johansen to make a dash across the ice floes with sledges and dogs. They left the *Fram* in latitude

84° N on 14 March 1895, provisioned for one hundred days, taking twenty-eight dogs and three sledges. In just under a month they reached their farthest north in latitude 86° 13′ from where the northern prospect was 'a veritable chaos of iceblocks'. There was no way of knowing the position of the *Fram*, so from there they made their way to Franz Joseph Land, averaging less than five miles a day over treacherous ice. After a tough winter in cold hibernation, they eventually stumbled upon the English Jackson-Harmsworth expedition on 17 June 1896, after a journey which, since leaving the *Fram*, had taken fifteen months. At Tromsö on 25 August 1896, Nansen and the *Fram* were happily re-united. His expedition, in the teeth of scepticism and discouragement, had drifted with the shifting expanse of polar ice across an unknown ocean – a courageous voyage inspired and conducted with consummate intelligence – a saga that will never be surpassed.

No further drifts were contemplated while the Pole remained a prize – a sporting challenge to the balloonist, the sledger and the airman. Even before Nansen's book *Farthest North* was published in 1897, a Swede by the name of Salomon Andrée had set off in a balloon from Spitzbergen with two companions to reach the North Pole, an attempt which cost them their lives.

The next attempt to reach the Pole was far more conventional than Andrée's expedition. It was an Italian effort led by Prince Luigi Amadeo of Savoy (the Duke of Abruzzi) – a distinguished Himalayan explorer, who had been inspired by Nansen's account of his sledge journey across the pack ice. The Italians set up their base on Franz Joseph Land in 1899, and the following spring made their assault. The Duke, being incapacitated by frost bite, delegated the command to Captain Cagni, and in three detachments, a total of nine men, thirteen sledges and a hundred and two dogs, set off across the pack ice. Cagni's detachment sledged north for forty-five days, reaching their farthest north on the 24th April in latitude 86° 34′ –

beating Nansen's record by 22 miles; but their return journey was hazardous in the extreme, and one of the detachments failed to reach the base. The Duke's conclusions from the experience of his men was that the Pole would never be reached from a base on Franz Joseph Land, and that future attempts should be made from the north of Ellesmere Island. This had already occurred to that most assiduous of all explorers, Robert E. Peary.

Peary, an American naval officer, was obsessed by the ambition to reach the North Pole and strove for twenty years until he saw the attainment of the Pole not only as his duty but also as his divine right. This very remarkable, even fanatical, man devoted meticulous attention to the planning of his campaigns; he developed and refined a technique of polar travel which enlisted whole villages of Eskimos as part of his military-style assault. He adopted Eskimo methods of sledging and used Eskimos as an integral part of his assault, dividing them into divisions under the leadership of competent white assistants. He was one of the first polar explorers to realize that the winter was the best time in which to travel, and on his final attempt at the Pole (at the age of fifty-three years) he set out from Cape Colombia, his land depot on the north coast of Ellesmere Island, on 22 February 1909.

It was in June of that same year, and only a few weeks before news reached the outside world that the Pole had been reached, that Harrison, an American, with somewhat limited polar experience, put before the Royal Geographical Society a proposal for crossing the Arctic Ocean by its longest axis, from Alaska to Spitzbergen. Harrison's plan was regarded by the Society as unfeasible and, like so many other plans that failed to get off the ground, was ignored by historians. I did not myself stumble upon this plan in time to benefit from its arguments, for by July 1967, when his proposal to the R.G.S. first came to my notice, I had just returned from a winter with the Eskimos in North-West Greenland and a dog-sledge journey of fourteen hundred miles from Greenland to Canada; this was part of the training programme for my own trans-Arctic expedition, the plans for which had not only been formulated four years previously but were by then operational.

Quite independently, we had arrived at the same general conclusion, namely, that 'if a ship will drift, a sledge party will drift'; at this point, however, our plans parted company, for his were based on an arithmetic which only he could understand:

I intend to start from Pullen Island with nine Eskimo and one hundred dogs to cross the Arctic Ocean to Spitzbergen where I expect to arrive nine hundred and twelve days later. I shall carry instruments for making soundings and other oceanographic observations – also instruments for surveying any lands that might be found.

The problem before me is as follows. I have seventy-two thousand pounds to move one hundred and fifty miles in one hundred and eighty-two days. I have a hundred dogs which, at the rate of ten dogs to a sledge, gives me ten sledges and each sledge will carry one thousand two hundred pounds. I propose, by means of relays and return journeys to move the whole of this material 0·82 miles each day. Ten sledges carrying one thousand two hundred pounds apiece will have to make six journeys in order to carry seventy-two thousand pounds. Therefore, I shall have to go 0·82 miles six times a day and back. This will amount to 9·02 miles per day. When I say ten sledges in use, I do not mean that I shall have only ten sledges. My entire supply of provisions will be carried on sixty sledges, and the dogs after drawing ten sledges for 0·82 of a mile will return for ten more loaded sledges. The dogs will therefore make only 4·92 miles each day dragging a load. If all goes well, by the end of six months, I shall have accomplished a hundred and fifty miles, and have eaten up eleven sledge loads. This diminution of eleven loads will make my future journey less arduous for in order to transfer the remaining fifty-eight thousand eight hundred pounds at the same rate of 0·82 miles per day, I shall only have to make five journeys per day. This reduces the amount traversed in a day from 9·02 to 7·38 miles per day. At this rate by the end of the first year, I shall have reached 75° north latitude and the amount to be carried will have been reduced from seventy-two thousand pounds to forty-five thousand six hundred pounds. In the second year, I hope to reach 87°30' north or to travel seven hundred and fifty miles. This will mean doing two miles per day, but on account of reduced loads, I shall have to make only four journeys, therefore, the average daily travel will be fourteen miles. This means that the dogs must travel eight miles per day loaded for at least six months. At the end of six months, another eleven sledge loads will be eaten which will leave twenty-seven loaded sledges. This reduces the to and fro journeys from four to three. This means ten miles a day or six with loaded sledges. During the next six months I hope to travel from latitude 85 north to Spitsbergen, a distance of seven hundred and fifty miles. This means doing four miles a day with sixteen sledge loads and a hundred dogs. For the first three months a journey of twelve miles per day will be necessary for some of the other dogs, but at the end of three months I shall only have ten and a half sledge loads left and a drift of two miles a day with me, which will mean travelling only two miles a day.

Harrison's proposal as it had been put before the Royal Geographical Society was fully discussed by a special committee, and whilst the consensus of opinion was that it was unpleasant to have to discourage so keen an explorer, they felt bound in this case to do so, and did. As Sir Lewis Beaumont pointed out, the proposal was 'contrary to anything that former Arctic experience justifies and, although of course one cannot

help admiring the daring and courage of any man who projects such an expedition and is willing to undertake it yet, when
the matter is referred to the Royal Geographical Society, and
I am asked, as one who has been to the Arctic, to give an
opinion, I cannot help feeling the responsibility of the Society
in this matter, coming to the conclusion that the idea does not
offer any reasonable hope of success'.

Far more hopeful of success were the supporters of Robert
Edwin Peary, whose party consisted of twenty-four men,
nineteen sledges and a hundred and thirty-three dogs. They had
good reason to expect Peary to succeed – it was undoubtedly
his last determined effort, his last chance to reach out and grasp
at glory.

Strictly according to plan, one by one his divisions had
turned back towards land until finally only Peary's division
remained. He claimed to have reached the North Pole on
6 April 1909, and to have covered the eight hundred unwit-
nessed miles between the farthest north camp of Bartlett (his
second in command) at latitude 87°47', to the Pole and back
along his tracks to Cape Colombia at an average speed of
thirty-four miles a day; during which, over a period of eight
consecutive days, he must have averaged at least forty-six miles
a day. Even giving Peary the benefit of the doubt by adding
only ten per cent to the total distance he covered during those
eight days to allow for detours (instead of the twenty-five
per cent which he found to be the additional distance which he
had had to travel on his previous expeditions across the ice
pack), these distances seem incredible. Captain Cagni's average
speed over a distance of six hundred and one miles of polar pack
was only 6·3 miles a day, and his best six consecutive days' travel
worked out at an average of 21·2 miles. Peary's average south
of the Bartlett Camp was considerably less, but again giving
him the benefit of the doubt and allowing in the calculations
for the southerly component of drifting pack ice giving him a
bonus of a few miles a day, his record for the return journey

still confounds all but his most ardent supporters and practically every polar expert.

Peary did not return home to the acclaim he had expected. A few days before he had sent his triumphant message 'Stars and Stripes nailed to the Pole!', a more dramatic announcement had astonished the world. Dr Frederick A. Cook, an experienced and respected American explorer, had declared that he, accompanied by two Eskimos, had reached the North Pole on 21 April 1908 – a year before Peary.

It was on 3 July 1907 that Cook had set out from Gloucester, Massachusetts, northward bound on a mission, the real purpose of which he had kept secret from all but his closest friends. He was a very experienced polar explorer. He had been the medical officer on board the Belgian Antarctic expedition of 1897–99, an expedition which had been the first to winter south of the Antarctic Circle, and on which Roald Amundsen (who was later to be conqueror of the South Pole) served as First Mate. That expedition had brought Cook considerable fame as an explorer, a scientist and a writer, and in 1907, after further increasing his stature as an explorer by making the first ascent of Mount McKinley, the highest mountain on the American Continent, he was easily persuaded by the millionaire sportsman, John R. Bradley, to organize a hunting expedition in North-West Greenland.

At Annoatok, a small Eskimo settlement in North-West Greenland, he went ashore and set up winter quarters, sending back with Bradley a letter addressed to the Explorers Club of New York, informing them that he would try for the Pole. He spent that winter with a German companion, Rudolph Francke, hunting and trading with the Eskimos, and on 19 February 1908, he, Francke, ten Eskimos, eleven sledges and one hundred and five dogs, set out across Smith Sound on a Poleward journey which was to take them in a north-westerly direction across Ellesmere Island through game territory discovered by Sverdrup to the northern tip of Axel Heiberg

Island. It was this part of Cook's route which I, Allan Gill and Roger Tufft had retraced during the fourteen hundred mile sledging journey which we made as part of the training programme for the British Trans-Arctic Expedition. But our guess as to how far he went from the northern tip of Axel Heiberg Island is not much better than anyone else's. After sending back all but four of his Eskimo companions, he claims he had set off across the pack ice in the direction of the Pole. Three days later, and about sixty miles north of Cape Stalworthy, he sent back two more Eskimos, and continued with his two Eskimo companions, Etukishook, Ahwelah and twenty-six dogs. He claims to have reached the North Pole on 21 April 1908, and during his return journey to have drifted off course and to have made a landfall one hundred and sixty miles to the south-west of Cape Stalworthy. It was then too late to get back on course and so take advantage of the caches of food he had left every fifty miles along his outward route, and he was obliged to continue due south. At Cape Sparbo in Jones Sound, he and his two companions suffered a miserable winter in a crude stone hut, and in the spring of 1909 continued their journey, manhauling their sledges up the east coast of Ellesmere Island and across Smith Sound to Annoatok. The journey had taken them fourteen months.

The Cook–Peary polar controversy is now fifty-eight years old and no nearer to being solved than it was in the first months of vicious and outrageous attacks which followed Peary's announcement on 6 September 1909 that he had reached the North Pole. Many millions of words have been written on the subject and many reputations staked. The Cook supporters invariably present almost incontrovertible arguments as to why Peary could not have reached the Pole – the Peary supporters, equally vehement, tear Cook's account to shreds. I cannot recall ever having read an assessment in which both claims were discredited, or for that matter any dispassionate verdict that both claims were acceptable.

Unsatisfactory though the final attainment of the Pole was, it at least extinguished for a time the burning torch at the top of the world. The Arctic could at last settle down to accept scientific expeditions unburdened by the lodestone of a geographic prize. There were of course other landmarks in the history of the Arctic, notably in the fields of flight and submarine voyages.

The Americans, Richard E. Byrd and Floyd Bennet, operating from their base in west Spitzbergen, claimed to have flown over the Pole on 29 April 1926; and a few days later the dirigible *Norge*, with a crew of sixteen men on board under the leadership of the famous Norwegian explorer, Roald Amundsen, made the first trans-Arctic flight from Spitzbergen to Alaska. In 1937, the North Pole, after being the goal of so many expeditions, became the starting-point of one: a Russian expedition under the leadership of Ivan Papanin was landed at the Pole, where they set up a scientific drifting station, which they occupied for eight months before being picked up off the east coast of Greenland after a drift of just over two thousand miles. This was an expedition of outstanding scientific merit and led to the establishment (after the Second World War) of several other drifting stations – both Russian and American. From these drifting stations, manned by scientists in relays throughout the years, the nature of the Arctic Basin has become a specialized study, and support for the drifting stations has become a practised technique. Regular commercial flights over the Arctic Ocean were inaugurated by Scandinavian Airlines System in November 1954, and were followed shortly afterwards by others; the first voyage of a nuclear-powered submarine across the Arctic Basin was successfully accomplished in August 1958 – the year that the Commonwealth Trans-Antarctic Expedition under Sir Vivian Fuchs made the first crossing of the Antarctic Continent. With the attainment of the North Pole and man's subsequent flights, drifts and submarine voyages, the skills of sledge travel, evolved through generations, slipped into disuse; and hardship, which for so long had been a factor in polar exploration, came to be regarded as an indication of foolhardiness in the field or incompetence on the part of the organizing committees. But less to the credit of intelligent men – so excited were scientists by advances in such fields as the geology of the ocean bed, geophysics and the dynamics of drifting ice – many of them failed to recognize at first any scientific value in a journey by dog sledge across the top of the world.

To complete the record of man's endeavour in the polar regions it seemed to me necessary to finish what had been only half accomplished – a trans-polar journey that in its historical setting would be the culmination of four centuries of human endeavour; a journey that would by definition be a pioneer journey, made possible by the marriage of the sledging technique with the most advanced form of logistic support, radios, homing beacons and satellite information on the weather and ice concentration. It was my belief that by walking across the top of the world we would learn more about the environment than we would by flying, submerging or stationing ourselves in a heated observatory on the ice. Such vision is seldom regarded at first as anything more than a dream, or an excuse for adventuring.

2 In the Footsteps of Amundsen

THREE YEARS WERE TO GO BY BETWEEN THE MEETING WITH THE HUNTER IN THE DESERTED MINE OF MOSKUSHAMN AND the sudden realization that the journey we had talked about was not only feasible but probably the most challenging journey left to man on the surface of this planet. I cannot claim that during those three years I nursed the dream of crossing the Arctic Ocean – on the contrary, for two of those three years I was obsessed by an ambition to reach the South Pole, and not until circumstances stopped me two hundred and seventy nautical miles short of that goal had I felt compelled, as Amundsen had felt half a century before, to switch my attentions to the other end of the earth.

Nor is it anything more than a coincidence that the latitude at which my three companions and I abandoned our winter quarters on the Arctic Ocean, and from which, with the odds stacked heavily against us, we had headed north for the Pole, was the same latitude from which in the south, seven years before, I had with three companions been forced to retreat in the face of odds that were in our favour. From that latitude, 85°30′ S, in ten days of hard sledging, we could have reached the South Pole on 27 January 1962 – fifty years and ten days after Captain Scott and his companions had stumbled upon the tent which Amundsen had left at the Pole a month earlier.

Our attainment of the South Pole would not have made history. I doubt if our achievement would have been given more prominence than a paragraph in the *Christchurch Star*, for we would have been at least the seventh overland party to have

reached the South Pole in the last fifty years. We were, however, not seeking the Pole for honours nor even for the purpose
of capitalizing on the fiftieth anniversary of the attainment of
the Pole by Amundsen and Scott. It simply made better sense
at the end of a season's work in the Queen Maud Range to
sledge for ten days across the featureless polar plateau to the
American South Pole station. From there we would be air-
lifted back to McMurdo Sound in a Hercules (which otherwise
would have returned to McMurdo empty), and would not
have to negotiate the ice falls of the Axel Heiberg Glacier –
which only Amundsen had travelled before us – in order to get
ourselves into a position from which a Dakota could lift us out.

I don't deny for a moment that the attainment of the South
Pole would have been for each of us a memorable experience;
indeed, for me it would have been the highpoint of a career
which had been carefully steered towards such a goal. Most of
my early life I had spent in Egypt and South Africa, where the
wide open spaces had excited and disturbed me; and at the
age of seventeen, impressed by an Army Recruiting brochure
and the persuasive arguments of my father, who had frequently
reminded me that every male relative on his side of the family
since Sir Harry Hotspur (1364-1403) had been soldiers by
profession, I had signed on for twenty-two years with the
Colours. I was taught by the Army how to navigate, and sent
out to Egypt; but in search of a more adventurous life I had,
after three years' service, been released and, with only £30 in
my pocket, had wandered back to Britain through the Middle
East and the Mediterranean countries drawing portraits for
my board and lodging. I had taken a job at Shoreham-by-Sea
as a surveyor and, despairing of travelling again, had lazed
away my free hours above the mudbanks of the estuary. My
hopes went seaward with the tide, and a church bell clanging
the hour of the day marked the passage of wasted time. I had
dreamt of ventures for which I seemed unqualified, and of
actions for which I was unfitted.

The turn of fate, when at last it came, had come with a gentle rush. It was, as I recall, a blustery day and the bus taking me to work was dank with the smell of steaming raincoats. I had paid my fare, lit my pipe, and had just closed my eyes when a newspaper fell into my lap from the overhead luggage-rack. It was open at the Public Appointments page, and as I wrestled to turn the page over, two advertisements caught my eye almost simultaneously: 'Surveyor required in Kenya' one said – and 'Expedition to Antarctica' said the other:

The Falkland Islands Dependency Survey which maintains isolated land bases in the Antarctic requires SURVEYORS. Candidates, SINGLE, must be keen young men of good education and of high physical standard, who have a genuine interest in Polar research and travel, and are willing to spend 30 months under conditions which are a test of character and resource. They must be competent to carry out surveying operations in the Antarctic. . . . Unqualified candidates who have had experience with the Ordnance Survey or the Royal Engineers Survey would be considered . . . salary in this case would be £330 rising to £420 per year. . . .

Unqualified in terms of the advertisement, I had sailed for Hope Bay, Antarctica, in 1955 and for the next two and a half years had lived a monastic life without religious exercise. There, we were a world of men in harmony with our environment – twelve men around a bunkhouse fire, or two men in a drumming tent, or one man in the solitude of summer-warmed hills. We saw a paradise in snowscapes and heard music in the wind, for we were young and on our long exploratory journeys we felt with the pride of youth that we were making history.

At the end of my first sojourn in the south I hitch-hiked alone back to Britain from Montevideo – a 15,000-mile journey during which time I lived and travelled rough. But I failed to work the Antarctic out of my system. I collapsed at home and nothing would induce me to talk about my travels. I harboured an almost inexplicable dread of stagnation, but was too tired and was too short of money to set out on another journey. I was then twenty-three and felt for the first time that I was growing old.

Eventually, committed to a lecture agency, I took the platform for an hour at a time as often as twenty-five times a week and talked about adventure – advocating escape to my listeners in church halls, schools, prisons, spastics homes and institutions for the insane, until it occurred to me that it was perhaps I that was in greater need of freedom, for even the inmates of Parkhurst seemed more content than myself.

On 1 May 1960 I broke out, joined my old sledging partner, Dr Hugh Simpson, and his wife Myrtle, and set out in an old Austin van loaded with gear on an expedition to the Arctic island of Spitzbergen. We drove through the magnificent mountain country of southern Norway early in the season. We were ahead of the tourists, and crossed the Arctic Circle through a stretch of country bleak and windswept where the snow lay rotting and small streams dribbled into rivers congealed with ice and slush. Leaving behind the great roaring waterfalls and boiling rapids, the spectacular gorges and the towering snow-capped mountains, we descended into fertile valleys, dotted with pretty Norwegian villages, and finally arrived at Tromsö, the township where Amundsen had set out on so many of his voyages.

There I received a cable asking me to go to Greenland to select and buy twelve huskies for the New Zealand Antarctic Expedition and transport them via the United States, Hawaii, Fiji and Christchurch to McMurdo Sound, Antarctica, where I was invited to join the expedition for two summers and a winter. I barely had time to get settled in at our base camp at Spitzbergen before I had to take the kayak back along the coast to catch the S.S. *Lyngen* sailing south from Longyearbyen on 19 June 1960.

My conversation with the hunter in Moskushamn, already described, had stirred in me nothing more than mild curiosity, for my ambitions by now were firmly focussed on the South Pole. Quite how I would set about seeking permission to divert a Government-sponsored field reconnaissance party from its field of operation across a featureless plateau to the Pole on a traverse which could serve no useful purpose, I had not stopped to consider. It was enough to be on my way to the Antarctic, and deeply involved with problems the solution to each of which would take me one step nearer my goal.

It was dark and raw when, some three weeks later, I stepped out of the aircraft on to a blustery tarmac at Sondre Stromfjord, Greenland, and ran for shelter towards a covered way which led directly into the hotel. Dawn crept slowly over the hills. A steel-grey runway, like a frozen lake, lay in shadow while the low sun washed the cliffs and fells and seeped down the hillside until it flooded the airstrip, brightened into the glare of daylight and drained all beauty from the landscape. Away in the distance the American airbase purred with activity. It was from there, on 26 October 1960, that I was to fly south with the dogs aboard a Globemaster of the U.S. Military Air Transport Service; and, though I did not know it then, it was to be through this same base, seven years later, that I was to stage the first 30,000 lbs of cargo aboard a Hercules of the Royal Air Force bound for Resolute Bay, the main staging depot for the supplies we would require during the first surface crossing of the Arctic Ocean.

For three days I paced the dusty tracks of that depressing place waiting for the weather to clear along the Greenland coast and the aircraft that eventually lifted me into a different world.

The houses of Egedesmine were small and steeply roofed – maroon boxes scattered around the rocky outcrops, each sitting squatly on its nest looking blankly at its neighbour through white window eyes. On the quay, Greenlanders stood sinking into rumpled trousers, their bow-legs like arched pillars supporting a paunch draped in scruffy sweaters, their shoulders drooping, hands in their pockets, their faces never far from smiling. I was to get to like these people in the course of time – but never fully to understand them. Sometimes impious, some-times sarcastic, but always in their hearts generous to the white man who is prepared to laugh at his own fumbling attempts to imitate their way of life and their techniques of travel, they are the twilight people, descendants of the 'Inuit', the 'real men', the Eskimaux, gathered together in settlements now for administrative convenience.

Of these settlements, there were only four on the west coast of Greenland from where I might have bought dogs. There was Qanaq, a village eighty miles north of Thule, the American strategic airbase: this had been my first choice, and was the village at which six years later I would spend the winter with Allan Gill and Roger Tufft, and from where we would pur-chase the dogs for the journey across the North Polar cap. There was Upernivik, south of Melville Bay; Umanak, tucked away in a pocket of good hunting territory a little further south; and finally there was Disco Bay where the settlement of Jakobshavn had a dog population of just over 3,000 – two dogs to every human being. Jakobshavn had supplied dogs for many polar expeditions in the past, and was the nearest of the four settle-ments to Søndre Strømfjord to where they had eventually to be shipped.

Jakobshavn, my choice of base by circumstance, was a tiny land-locked harbour surrounded by low craggy hills under a dusting of summer snow. At the head of the little harbour which was like a giant bird-bath, its water sprinkled with brash ice and sludge and tide-marked with a pale ochre stain, window-less warehouses stood with their foundations in the water, as if the hills had pushed them to the very edge. They were in the shadow of the hills behind them, a shadow which lay across the ice-choked water and stained the brash and sludge pale blue;

in the sunlight, the ice glistened like flashing diamonds. Away from the water's edge, on each bald rock, small box-like huts and houses stood.

The villagers of Jakobshavn were delightful old rogues to deal with when it came to buying dogs, and some of my happiest recollections of Greenland are of the wranglings between the dog-owners and myself through my two interpreters. I often received the most incongruous answers to questions that were presumably lost in the translation, but by drawing portraits of the dog-owners and priming them just before the final purchase with a crate of beer, I eventually got the dogs I wanted. Whether the Greenlanders fully understood why I needed those dogs or to where I was taking them, there was no way of knowing. It was probably beyond their comprehension that within ten days those dogs would be transported through 160 degrees of latitude, from autumn into spring, and within two weeks would be hauling a sledge in a vast and magnificent Antarctic setting not ten miles from the farthest southern latitude reached by Scott, Shackleton and Wilson in 1902.

During that first summer with the New Zealanders in the Antarctic, I spent two months in the field with the dogs I had brought from Greenland, and the map that resulted covered 10,000 square miles of previously unexplored country in the Nimrod Glacier region. The season was a great success, a credit to everyone connected with it; but it was the most boring and frustrating two months I had ever spent in the South, for by comparison with the Graham Land region of the Antarctic where I had spent two and a half years with a British expedition, the weather and terrain in the New Zealand sector of Antarctica seemed comfortable and safe. Had I not by that time realized the possibilities of a tremendous field season in the Queen Maud Range during the austral summer of 1961-62 which I had visions of climaxing with a dash to the South Pole, I would seriously have considered resigning from the Expedition, for I felt I was wasting precious time. I could see all around me during that first season signs that within a few years there would be nothing left to explore in the Antarctic. Most of the American field parties were using huge tracked vehicles which towed sledge-caravans, the New Zealanders were already considering replacing the dogs with motorized sledges, there was a first-order survey triangulation planned for the following season using turbo-prop helicopters to put the surveyors on the mountain summits, and the photographic coverage of the Continent was steadily blacking in the chart on which the missions were plotted. The days of dog sledging in the Antarctic were almost over – there was, as I saw it, one last season only in which any major journey could be made, and one last opportunity to take dogs to the South Pole.

On the 12th May, after much careful thought and discussion with the Americans at McMurdo, I sent a telegram to Mr Markham, the Director of the Antarctic Division of the Department of Scientific and Industrial Research in Wellington, New Zealand, proposing a four-man expedition to the area east of the Beardmore Glacier. I was not too specific about the area because the only maps I had, indeed the only maps that existed, were those of Shackleton and Scott, neither of which extended beyond the range that walled the east side of the glacier. My plan was for a dog-sledging party, supported by aircraft, ascending the area left blank on Scott's map from the Shelf Ice to the polar plateau where we would meet the Dominion range. This range did not look at all formidable as a barrier to the polar plateau on either Scott's or Shackleton's maps – it was drawn in on both of them like a narrow strip of cumulus cloud which petered out. I proposed to finish the map (which I guessed would cover about 20,000 square miles) at the tail of that range, and then head due south for the Pole. The dash I saw as a fitting celebration of the fiftieth anniversary of the attainment of the South Pole and as a sensible way of getting back to McMurdo, for my friends in VX-6 Squadron (the U.S. Navy's crack support-reconnaissance squadron) had assured me that there would be no objection to loading my party aboard an empty Hercules aircraft returning from the American South Pole Station at that time of the year. Mr Markham's reply was two weeks in coming:' Your initiative and enthusiasm to enlarge next season's programme and capitalize on Scott anniversary appreciated and commended, however . . .' – the telegram went on to tear my proposal to shreds, and pointed out that I had not yet been appointed leader. He did, however, kindly offer to consider my proposal as an application for the post 'along with others received'.

Mid-winter came in with its parties and gaudy bunting, paper hats and clean white shirts, and in no time at all it seemed we were racing towards spring. The survey office and the sledge workshop came alive with atmosphere. The smell of wood and linseed oil, rope and canvas, dogs, dope, blubber, tobacco; the clutter of brightly coloured boxes, half-built sledges, field rations bulging in polythene bags; the soft rumble of the generators in the nearby hut and the purring of the fans; the classical symphonies on the tape-recorder, the buzz of conversation, and the chatter of the sewing machine built up an atmosphere of urgency, of expectation, of momentum, which attracted men to it like a magnet. It was a pocket of the old-fashioned expedition spirit in a metal survival machine that was Scott Base, where through its sledging chattels, smells and sounds, the base party felt themselves being drawn into the slipstream of the field men who had broken away to race towards spring.

A dead sky flushed with a rosy hue. A pink moon floated full and slow on its last circuits of a silent world. The air temperature sank to − 72°F. It was still, very still. Each breath we drew in was cold, brittle steel. The air seemed to crack if we walked through it too quickly. The sledges were ready, the food boxes were packed and careful lists of equipment prepared. At noon each day, as we worked down at the dog lines, the shadow of Mount Erebus reached over us. The northern horizon was a brilliant yellow – the sea ice in McMurdo Sound was a green-grey table set to receive the first grazing rays of the returning sun.

Each day at noon the sun curved nearer – it caught White Island to our south in a flush of rose, whilst the shelf ice in the foreground was still in the shadow of the earth; it was like a steel bar heated by a furnace, thrust across our southern horizon – and the air temperature soared.

We saw our first glimpse of the sun at Scott Base on the 3rd September – five months after it had set behind Mount Erebus – but we were pinned at base for almost a week by the first blast of storms that heralded summer, and it was not until the 11th September that we were able to set off with our teams of dogs on a training run north to visit the old huts of Shackleton and Scott. It was early in the morning, the sun had not cleared Hut Point Peninsula but it blazed past Cape Armitage like a curtain of gold and etched a rim about Observation Hill on which stands a cross in memory of Scott and his four gallant companions. It was cold in the shadow and the scene was stark, but as we reached Cape Armitage and cut into the sunlight it burst into orange flame. Some six hours later we drove the dogs above the tide crack and camped on a narrow ledge of snow about sixty yards from the hut in which Captain Scott had passed the winter of 1911. They had during that winter produced two volumes of the *South Polar Times*, the second appearing on the 8th September. Their ghosts perhaps were still reading the second volume when we barged into the hut fifty years later, our eyes unaccustomed to the dim interior, for only a fading glow was framed at the two windows at the far end of the hut. We bumped into a table and the creak of floorboards and leaping shadows brought the hut alive with movement. It was cold and eerie, but we stayed close together and passed on to the wardroom, once separated from the messdeck by a pile of food cases through which a door-size gap gave access. Chairs sat to attention at the long, bare, wardroom table; behind them the cubicles, ramshackle structures stained with blubber and smoke, cluttered with remnants of worn-out clothing, grimy and musty. In the right-hand far corner of the old hut was the science lab. In the left-hand far corner we found Scott's cubicle, and as we sat on Wilson's bunk looking across the chart table we could visualize Captain Scott writing his journal fifty years before.

That night in the hut they had been working hard on the final preparations for their spring journeys: 'a very demon of unrest seemed to stir them to effort and there is now not a single man who is not striving his utmost . . .' (from *Captain Scott*, Vol. 1, 1914, page 406). The candle flame leapt and its glow penetrated the darkness. I shielded its glow with my hand and moved forward slowly. Shadows crept around the room; the pale light moved over the sleeping-bags bulging on bunks, breathing it seemed, fusty with age. I gathered up an armful of magazines, disturbing an odour which rose off them; and around the hut, beyond the weak pool of light, groans came like whispers of reproach. Two chairs had been moved to one side; they relaxed at an angle compared with the rest, so I gave them a wide berth and brushed against two furry mitts dangling limply from the side of a bunk and stubbed my foot against something lying on the floor. The shadows circled as I moved towards the door; they seemed to float just out of reach and creep up behind me and rest on my back.

Shackleton's hut was no less eerie. Time was turned back half a century by the adventurous spirits that dwelt in that place, but in a way it was a stimulating experience; it caught me that day with the rising Pole fever. I was called back to base by radio on the eve of 20 October 1961. I had to get back to Scott Base within a few hours to join an aircraft which was to make a reconnaissance flight of 1,600 miles over the area in which I would be working during the coming season.

We walked around with reverence, high up in the air, while the flight engineer and navigator studied dials and filled up forms. Warm air breathed from the mouth-like vents of the aircraft. Hours went by and mountain ranges came and went until the horizon seemed to sink and the aircraft changed its course. The broad white road of the Beardmore Glacier crawled away from under the starboard wing, between bold mountains climbing up to the polar plateau, hazy in the distance. Flying along the foothills of the Queen Maud Range we lost ourselves on the navigator's map. It was dotted with outlines of mis-shapen glaciers. We were looking for one of them in particular – the Axel Heiberg, Amundsen's route to the polar plateau – but for what purpose I cannot recall, for at that time we had not considered using it as a route ourselves. The Shackleton Glacier was easily identified, even with the rough sketch-map which was our guide; a raking, naked monster it looked. We counted the glaciers marked to its east, then turned up the Strom Glacier, the engines roaring with extra power. Skimming a massif, we caught our breath. The faces of rock and yawning blue chasms, snow fields and chaotic icefalls, spurs and ridges, opaque shadows and brilliant sun-drenched domes of snow slipped past our steamy windows. Not one of us had any idea where we were and it was not until many months later, when showing colour slides in New Zealand, that I realized that on that day we had flown right over the Axel Heiberg Glacier.

The aircraft landed at the McMurdo airstrip some hours later and I was little wiser about my new area, other than the knowledge that the landing spot was 600 miles from base. I staggered back to Scott Base and started my final bid to gather support for the dash for the Pole.

There had been a meeting of the Scientific Committee on Antarctic Research a few weeks before in Wellington, and its august members had flown to McMurdo as guests of Rear Admiral Tyree. Dressed all alike, they were blasted into the air each day, and flown to the four corners of the Antarctic and back in time for dinner. They gave my plan a sympathetic hearing; and all agreed with Sir Vivian Fuchs, who spent three days with us at Scott Base surrounded by admirers, that it would be more dangerous to descend from the plateau than to sledge across it to the American station at the South Pole from where I could be safely transported back to base. Through their influential support I *almost* got permission. Only Athyl Roberts, the base leader at Scott Base, remained unconvinced and begged me not to press my Pole dash further.

On my last night at Scott Base, before my last season in the Antarctic, I was invited to Flag Quarters at McMurdo to discuss my plans with Admiral Tyree. With disarming sincerity he admitted that he would have liked to see my team make the journey to the Pole on the fiftieth anniversary of a heroic struggle, but times had changed and search and rescue in the event of any mishap would involve more men than he could spare at so late a date in the summer season.

My plan for the exploration of the Queen Maud Range had changed somewhat since my first conception of the idea. It was now my intention to be landed with sixty days' supply of food and equipment at the head of the Beardmore Glacier. From here we would sledge to the east along the plateau edge, climbing all the highest peaks and surveying the country below us. In this way we hoped to cover an area of some 20,000 square miles of unexplored country with maps of a very high standard.

On 16 January 1962 – fifty years to the day after Captain Scott and his four companions had learnt for the first time that they had been forestalled at the South Pole by Amundsen's party – we made the first ascent of Mount Fritdtjof Nansen. 'Great God! This is an awful place,' Scott wrote in his diary of 17 January 1912, 'and terrible enough for us to have laboured to it without the reward of priority'. Those immortal words were singing in my ears during the seventeen hours we were on that 13,330-foot mountain, cringing in the stabbing wind, struggling to do our survey, stopping every few minutes to blow into our gloved hands and massage our stiff bodies.The misery and exhaustion we suffered dug deeply into our reserves, and the long trudge back down to camp almost claimed the four of us. It was less windy down below and the sun was soothing, but in spite of the risks of resting we were compelled to lie down every few yards. Our last rest was only a hundred yards from the tents, which we reached at 4.30 on the morning of the 17th January.

The idea of descending Amundsen's route on the Axel Heiberg Glacier had occurred to me on New Year's Eve. It had seemed to me that it would be a fitting climax to a season spent mapping the area between Scott's route to the Pole, and Amundsen's route through the Queen Maud Range, to re-discover the route taken by Amundsen down the Axel Heiberg Glacier.

Amundsen's route on the glacier had been a triumph of courage, experience and good sportsmanship. The object of his expedition had been to beat Scott to the South Pole. On the face of it, there was no reason why Amundsen should not have driven his dog teams directly from his base camp to the Beardmore Glacier – a route to the polar plateau already discovered and pioneered by Shackleton. There was no written rule forbidding Amundsen to use the Beardmore route. But the idea of using the same route as Scott had scarcely occurred to him. In his book, Amundsen says: 'Scott had announced that he was going to take Shackleton's route, and that decided the matter. During our long stay at Framheim not one of us ever hinted at the possibility of such a course. Without discussion Scott's route had been declared out of bounds' (Amundsen, Roald, *The South Pole*, Vol. I, 1912, p. 52).

By sledging due south, he ran the risk of finding his path barred by an unbroken chain of mountains; and since he had no ulterior scientific motive for his expedition, as had Scott, the success or failure of Amundsen's expedition depended on finding a new route to the polar plateau. This was a challenge which Amundsen and his companions had accepted, and by tackling the Axel Heiberg Glacier, which from every angle looks appalling as a sledging route, they proved themselves masters of their own fate.

The Beardmore Glacier, as seen from Mount Hope, had given Shackleton and his companions the opposite impression. It stretched out before them like a mighty highway to the Pole. The glacier was 140 miles long and its gradient was gentle, rising to only 7,800 feet at the plateau. Even its direction was favourable, for the first half of the climb lay due south and the second half lay south-west. But whereas it took Scott and his companions fourteen days to manhaul their heavy sledges up this previously explored and relatively straight-forward route to an altitude of 7,800 feet, it had taken Amundsen only four days, including reconnoitring, to climb to an altitude of 10,600 feet. His achievement was even more remarkable because he took a short-cut through the mountains, climbing to 4,550 feet and making two descents totalling 3,335 feet before he even got on to the Axel Heiberg Glacier. His total climb up the glacier amounted to 13,250 feet, and his total climbing from the time he left the ice shelf to the time he returned from the Pole was 19,590 feet as against the 11,470 feet climbed by Scott's party.

Amundsen's account of his descent of the Axel Heiberg Glacier was undramatic; it created the impression that he had found an easy route to the polar plateau. Even the errors he made on the glacier did not seem unduly to hinder his progress. It was a race he was running for the South Pole: he had been forestalled at the North Pole by Dr Frederick A. Cook and Commander Robert E. Peary, and he could not afford to be beaten at the South Pole by Scott. It had been his lifelong dream to conquer the North Pole but by an incredible set of circumstances he had found himself instead at the South Pole on 14 December 1911. I can understand his feelings, having experienced something of the same myself.

Amundsen's trip down the glacier on his return from the Pole was so uneventful and straightforward that it barely gets a mention in his book, and yet by reading between the lines of this master of understatement I can see how breathtaking that trip must have been. He covers the crux of the descent with no more than these words: 'On the ridge where the descent to the Glacier began we halted to make our preparations. Brakes were put under the sledges, and our two ski sticks were fastened together to make one strong one; we would have to be able to stop instantly if surprised by a crevasse as we were going. We ski runners went in front. The going was ideal here on the steep slope, just enough loose snow to give one good steering on ski. We went whizzing down, and it was not many minutes before we were on the Heiburg Glacier' (Amundsen, Vol. II, 1912, p. 157).

On 20 January 1960, it was an overcast day, oppressive with tension, shadowless, still. The brink of the first drop we could not see. Amundsen had called it the 'severe steep slope' and I skied towards it to check it for myself, while my companions sorted out the gear we would take down with us on our reconnaissance. We dared not commit ourselves to the glacier with our full loads as we might have met an impasse and had to return; nor could we risk an accident on the glacier, for we had not been given permission to attempt the descent. It had to be done in less than four days. We had no intention of taking the radio, which weighed almost seventy pounds, and four days off the air was a mute clarion call for search and rescue to begin. A route had to be flagged through the icefalls and we had to be back on the plateau by 7.30 p.m. on the 24th January.

At the edge of the drop I waited; and as the spears of weak sunlight fell through the rotting cloak of thick cloud overhead and pierced the soft mists in the basin, I skied cautiously over the brink. At first I skied too slowly to feel the wind of movement; but the slightest ripple in the surface looked in that spectral light like a gash – the livid lip of a crevasse – and distracted, I went sweeping past them, the slope taking charge and tilting me in a gliding plummet. I descended just over 1,000 feet – the run was safe – but it took me an hour and a quarter to climb back up to the camp.

We descended with the sledges and dogs to a point about halfway down the glacier from where two of my party returned to the plateau summit, while Vic McGregor and I skied on down the icefalls of the Axel Heiberg into the cwm. Thundering avalanches, exploding white cushions of snow, settled and stained the floor with debris. We studied the icefalls through binoculars for almost an hour trying to imagine a route, but scale was impossible to judge. We were at that point, at least 2,000 feet above the chaotic ice, that was the crux of Amundsen's route. We had no hope of finding a way; but in order to get some photographs amongst those spectacular icefalls, we had set off and free skied down a switchback fall of 1,500 feet to the middle terrace of the icefalls. Carefully working our way down, we reached a point at 6.30 a.m. from where we felt fairly confident that the remainder of the glacier route would be feasible for the teams of dogs. The altitude at that spot was just under 3,000 feet – we were 6,000 feet below our depot on the polar plateau.

On our way back up the icefalls we stuck in marker flags at every change of direction so that on our descent later with the dog teams, should the weather be against us, we would be able to feel our way between the crevasses by taking a straight line route from one marker flag to the next. Each crevasse bridge we proved and tested thoroughly. We could get down with the dog teams, I felt sure.

On arriving back at the plateau summit I sent out by morse a radio message to Scott Base jubilantly announcing that we had flagged a route through the icefalls of the Axel Heiberg and asking for official permission to descend the glacier in order to be picked up from the Ice Shelf by a Dakota. We felt sure this permission would be given for there were no suitable landing sites on the polar plateau within a hundred miles of our camp. My claim that we had descended the icefalls of the Axel Heiberg Glacier was disbelieved at Scott Base, McMurdo and in Wellington, where the details were analysed by polar experts. How Amundsen would have laughed if he could have seen us, beating our knees with frustration beside a radio set, listening to garbled reports of conferences held between our superiors on whether or not to give us permission to descend the glacier. How very different was the heroic age of polar exploration! In those days a party many hundreds of miles from base and without radio could take their calculated risks with almost gay abandon. No longer are polar explorers permitted to face their dangers alone, nor are they permitted to go off the air and take their calculated risks in peace and quiet. Radio, that wonderful piece of apparatus, had become our burden.

With only two days' food left, and with the winds cooling the polar plateau, our situation was absurd. We trudged into head-winds as long as we could tolerate it, and camped as our flesh began to freeze. Our faces became sheets of ice, our hands and feet died as fatigue slowed our progress to a halt. Unconscious habits pitched our camps; half-conscious bodies crawled inside the tents. Frozen fingers switched on the radio. Our sledging time crept out of phase as blizzards pinned us to one spot. But eventually on 1 February 1962, fifty years and one month after Amundsen and his companions had descended the Axel Heiberg Glacier, we left that infernal plateau with loads of nearly nine hundred pounds on each sledge and sank into a warm, windless, cosy pocket. Our camp was pitched less than a mile from Amundsen's camp of 4 January 1912, but the following morning my radio temporarily packed up. I had been given permission to descend the glacier provided that I made contact with base by radio no less than three times a day! On the 5th of February, to our delight, we discovered that we had camped on almost the exact location of Amundsen's camp-site of 18 November 1911 and 5 January 1912. We made this discovery when comparing photographs in Amundsen's book. On which of those dates he took those photographs we could not be sure, but by using them to get a photographic resection, we found that we could not move more than a hundred feet in any direction without upsetting the comparison between the scenery and Amundsen's photographs. We saved our celebration for the evening of the 5th of February, by which time we had sledged ten miles out along the glacier towards the mouth, and had contacted Base with the news that we had safely descended the glacier and were heading for the Shelf Ice to look for a pick-up point. We had made a map covering 22,000 square miles of the Beardmore Glacier and the Queen Maud Range. It had been a successful season and the glow of its climax was still fresh.

Six and a half years had passed since I had sat above the mud banks of an estuary near Shoreham-by-Sea frustrated by the dreams of youth which had no pilot, no set course, no destination this side of the horizon. But the horizon pulled more strongly from the foot of the Axel Heiberg Glacier than ever it had done at the tender age of twenty.

To the north the world lay; there was nothing to the south except a completed journey and the Pole which had now, prohibited to me, lost its appeal. To the north, the Ross Ice Shelf spread out like a mighty ocean. From beneath our feet to the horizon, and six hundred miles beyond to the nearest habitation, the frozen rollers heaved across an expanse of desolation. To the north lay my future – to the south, my past. I saw those years as paintings, uncompleted canvasses – each a different scene, all painted by the same unskilled hand. There were pictures of the desert there, the Andes and the Arctic, each one evoking memories of unfulfilled ambitions. But eighteen months were to go by before I had completed my maps in New Zealand, travelled back to England, and felt once again the frustration from which grew the excitement of a new idea.

3 The Plan

I HAD BEEN STUDYING THE SEPTEMBER 1957 ISSUE OF THE *Polar Record* – THE JOURNAL OF THE SCOTT POLAR RESEARCH Institute. The particular page which had caught my eye had a map of the Arctic Ocean on which were plotted the tracks of several drifting stations. I did a little research and, after plotting on the same map the tracks of the American scientific drifting stations, was intrigued to find that the ice circulation formed a pattern which broadly divided into two currents: one was evidently a slow-moving current drifting clockwise in the western half of the Arctic Ocean; the other, a faster moving current, originated north of the New Siberian Islands, flowed over the North Pole and out of the Arctic Ocean between Spitzbergen and north-east Greenland.

It occurred to me that a party of four men and three teams of dogs, by setting out from Point Barrow, Alaska, and sledging via the North Pole to north-east Greenland, would so benefit from the drift of the pack ice that they would be able to maintain an average of fourteen miles a day and complete the trans-Arctic journey in a hundred and thirty days. I had not taken into account in those first rough calculations that the 1,850-mile airline route from Barrow to north-east Greenland would, over the polar pack, be increased by thirty per cent or more, nor had I at that time studied the records of previous explorers who had attempted to reach the North Pole. Perhaps it was just as well, for had I realized how many years of hard work, frustration and disappointment lay ahead, I might never have taken my rough plans to Sir Vivian Fuchs on 20 April 1964.

The plan was a fumbling one and was to be modified many times over in the next couple of years. Even so, it was feasible enough to capture Sir Vivian's interest, for, as a result of my first quick study of the records of previous explorers, I had modified my original plan. I realized that a dash of a hundred and thirty days was impracticable, and had proposed a journey lasting sixteen months during which, throughout the period of continuous darkness, the party would conduct a programme of scientific research. My intention in the proposal I put before Sir Vivian had been to set off from Barrow, Alaska, on 1 August 1966. This I later advanced to April Fools' Day, 1966, and on 29 December 1964 I wrote to the Director of the Royal Geographical Society and to Sir Raymond Priestley, a veteran on Shackleton's and Scott's Antarctic Expeditions, offering my plan for criticism.

I had for some months been working full-time on the plans and writing hundreds of letters to polar experts all over the world from a tiny room in my parents' home which I had converted into an office. There I had my polar library and an assortment of souvenirs, a telephone, a set of box-files, *Burke's Peerage*, and a dictionary of synonyms. I had already spent eighteen months in that office, working on maps and papers resulting from my last Antarctic expedition, and on a book entitled *A World of Men*. It was a monastic existence I lived. I hardly knew anyone in Lichfield where we lived, and sorties from my office were seldom farther than the half-mile walk to the Post Office. I did not speak to my barber, nor did I chat to the bartender. I lived on money borrowed from the bank on the security of literary contracts, and on money borrowed from friends on no security at all.

Early in 1965 I was invited to visit Dr Max E. Britton at the Office of Naval Research in Washington, D.C., and to discuss my plans with Max C. Brewer at the Arctic Research Labor-

atory, Barrow, Alaska; so, with a grant of £200 from the
Royal Geographical Society, together with an 'advance on
future earnings' from my literary agent, I packed a suitcase and
flew to New York.

Five weeks later I was back in England, having visited in that
time all the major cities and centres of Polar Research in the
United States, Canada and the Scandinavian countries, including the outpost of Barrow, Alaska, from where I intended
starting out on the trans-Arctic journey. I had even flown in a
DC-8 jet over the Arctic Ocean by a route similar to that which
I proposed taking with dog teams in 1966-67. By the time I
got back to Britain, however, I was deeply in debt, and obliged
to sell my souvenirs and several volumes from my polar library.
I badly needed money to cover my expenses during the following period of two months in which I prepared a detailed
plan running to about twenty thousand words. This *thesis* was
in the form of a proposal to the Royal Geographical Society.
It was dated 20 July 1965.

Almost three months went by before the Society were able
to consider that proposal, for most of the members of the
Expeditions Committee were away on holiday; however, a
sub-Committee of polar experts was convened and on the
11th October I was thoroughly interrogated. The result was a
resolution couched in sympathetic terms: '. . . that the Expeditions Committee should recommend support of the trans-
Arctic Expedition as a well-planned and feasible, adventurous,
pioneer journey though with only very slight scientific content'.
But this resolution, after being thoroughly debated by the full
Committee on the 1st November, was rejected on the grounds
that expeditions supported by the Royal Geographical Society
should show some scientific or technological dividends, and
that the Society would not be justified in backing a purely
adventurous enterprise, more especially as doubts had been
expressed about my ability to raise sufficient financial support
in the short time available.

That rejection was shattering. I had gone to them with a plan for the attainment of what I considered to be a 'horizontal Everest'. I had read only two days before Bjørn Staib's book *On Skis Towards the North Pole* – a racy account of an abortive attempt by the Norwegian to make the first crossing of the Arctic Ocean, which could not fail to excite the interest of a few adventurous young men. His assault had failed because he had allowed himself insufficient time; but he was a bold young man for whom I have considerable respect, and I felt certain there were others like him poring over maps of the polar basin and reading polar books. The Staib North Pole Expedition was a brave expression of youthful enterprise – it was inevitable that there would be others.

That rejection put me, on the face of it, in a worse position than any in which I had been during the past three years, for my personal debts were now in the region of £3,000. The support of the Royal Geographical Society was to have been my certificate of competence from which the financial backing of the venture would have received its initial impetus. Had I sought the support of private patrons I might have raised the backing independently of the Royal Geographical Society – indeed, I had been advised strongly to do so by several sympathetic friends – but so confident had I been that the Society would support my proposed expedition, I had disregarded them.

So began the long hard slog all over again, practically from scratch. Why I didn't give up there and then I am not sure – perhaps it was in an effort to salvage three years of wasted work that I went back to my office desk and began typing hundreds of letters.

I worked through the long list of men who had received medals or awards from the Royal Geographical Society, and compared my list with *Who's Who* to see if any of them were still alive. Fifteen hours a day I put in at that typewriter, until the pit of my back was aching and my fingertips were as hard as hammers. But the encouragement I received was exhilarating.

Foremost amongst those who supported me were Sir Vivian Fuchs, the leader of the Commonwealth Trans-Antarctic Expedition of 1955-58, and my Literary Agent George Greenfield. My struggles and frustrations they frequently discussed over a beer after their weekly game of squash; but it was seldom that I saw them, for I could not afford the rail fare to London – one trip to London was equivalent to three hundred fourpenny stamps or eighty airmail letters to Canada or the United States, and it was postage and phone calls that had the priority during that period.

How my parents suffered! I would occasionally catch them watching me or whispering to each other. They would stand aside as I breezed through the house in my daily race to catch the last post, or wait tense and quietly as I read my mail over breakfast every morning. It was rarely I had any visitors, but on the odd occasions when Dennis Kershaw turned up, the relief of tension was overwhelming. Dennis was one of my closest friends – I had sailed south with him on the maiden southern cruise of the *Royal Research Ship Shackleton* way back in 1955. We had spent two and a half years in the Antarctic on separate expeditions, and had re-united on the high plateau that caps the spine of Graham Land after several months of hard physical toil and short rations. But we seldom reminisced about the South where we had spent our happiest years, or about South America through which we had separately hitch-hiked on our long journey back to Britain. We talked only about the present and the future – the struggle for the support of a dream, or about his wife and kids and cricket, or about my monastic existence of which he was always critical. But there was no question in my mind of postponing the Expedition by taking a part-time job, for to give any job full concentration I had to work full time.

The turning-point in the affairs of the Expedition, when at

last it came, was surprisingly undramatic. It occurred on 25 February 1966. I had lunched with George Greenfield and together we had gone along to visit Sir Vivian Fuchs at his office. A bulging file of letters from well-wishers and polar explorers lay unopened on the floor, for although those letters had raised my hopes when first I received them it had occurred to me for perhaps the first time that more positive support was needed to set the plans in motion. We decided to invite a few eminent gentlemen to form an advisory committee; but in spite of the congenial company of my two friends, or perhaps because of it, I had admitted to being depressed. I well remember the telling-off George gave me during the taxi ride back to his office: 'Don't admit,' he advised me, 'even to your closest friends, that you have the slightest doubt in your own abilities.'

Ten days later, as a result of that talk with George and Sir Vivian, I travelled down to London to meet at Sir Vivian's office Sir Miles Clifford, a former Governor of the Falkland Islands, and a member of the committee of Sir Vivian Fuchs' Trans-Antarctic Expedition. I was over two hours late for the meeting because of some major railway reconstruction in the Midlands which had disrupted the entire network of rail services, and, although no fault of mine, I felt wretched about having kept them waiting. I recall vividly the advice of Eleanor Honnywill, Sir Vivian's personal secretary, the moment before I went into the room: 'Stand up straight, take a deep breath, pull your shoulders back – now walk boldly in.'

The interview was brief, almost curt. My plan which had been carefully studied by Sir Miles was tested with a few searching questions, and in less than half an hour it was over – Sir Miles was invited to act as Chairman of a Committee whose object would be to help launch the Expedition.

Some very eminent men rallied to the cause and by the middle of June, 1966, our Committee was formed. Colonel Andrew Croft, the Arctic explorer, and Rear-Admiral Sir Edmund Irving, the Hydrographer to the Navy, were the first

First day out. Polar bear shot by Eskimo hunter, *right*

Second day out. Typical ice conditions near Alaskan coast

Rough ice before reaching polar pack ice

Shear zone: a newly opened crack

Mush ice

Travelling on rough ice

Cutting route across rift in old polar ice

Sledge repairs

Beethoven, Fritz's lead dog

Wally's team on well-developed frost flowers

Pressured old polar ice

Camp, April 1968

At top: A wide lead bars the way.
Left: Converting sledge to boat
with PVC. *Right:* Boat launched,
with dogs and supplies

Air drop by R.C.A.F.

to respond to the invitation. Both of them I had known for some time; they had supported me at meetings with the Royal Geographical Society and had often encouraged me when I was depressed. Mr Pirie-Gordon, Director of Glyn Mills Bank, I had not previously met, although I had known of him for several years. He had been Honorary Treasurer of every major expedition that had left Great Britain in the last decade, and Honorary Treasurer of the Royal Geographical Society whose support I still sorely needed. He, however, was not the only banker on our Committee; Alan Tritton, the local Director of Barclays Bank in Lombard Street, had joined us. Alan, the youngest member of the Committee, had been south with the British Antarctic Expedition of 1952-54. We were honoured also to have with us Lord Hunt, the leader of the British Expedition which had made the first ascent of Mount Everest in 1953, and Sir Arthur Porritt, then Sergeant-Surgeon to the Queen, now Governor-General of New Zealand. But this group of men, who, together with George Greenfield, were in due course to become a closely knit and very select 'club' which met on an average every three weeks, had not, at the time of my third meeting with the R.G.S. Expeditions Committee, joined forces, and but for the encouragement of a few close friends I was obliged once more to propose my expedition without the backing of an organization, let alone the financial backing of £54,000 – the figure which I estimated was required to launch the venture.

I had entered the conference room of the R.G.S. on the 18th April feeling truculent, for I believed it more than likely that they would reject my proposal yet again. But within a few minutes I sensed a sympathetic atmosphere, and by the time I left I was almost certain that I had at last the approval of the Society – an approval confirmed later by the pleasant express-ions and, in some cases, even the smiles of the members of the Committee as they walked in threes and fours through the hall to the gentlemen's cloakroom (where I had hung about for

C

almost half an hour knowing that I would, if I waited long enough, meet them as they came in to collect their bowler hats).

From time to time special advisers were called in at our Committee meetings, and some of them in due course joined George as *ex-officio* members. Mr Gordon Johnstone, the Expedition's auditor, was one of them; Squadron-Leader Freddie Church was another. We were joined, too, at a much later stage by Prince Yuri Galitzine; but it was Sir Vivian who throughout the development of the Expedition was anchorman and principal counsellor. It was his confidence in the plan that had helped to persuade some of the members of the Committee to join, and it was in his office that we held our first meeting on 9 June 1966.

That meeting was something of an ordeal. Of the eight men who had gathered to help me, I had previously met only four. Not unnaturally my plan and I were subjected to close scrutiny, but in less than two hours they had the measure of the situation and resolved that we should form a Company Limited by Guarantee, and that the Memorandum and Articles of Association should be so worded that the Expedition would be eligible for charitable status. It was agreed that at least for the time being we should not make a public appeal for funds, but should finance the first part of the Expedition plan – the training programme in North-West Greenland – on the advances on copyrights and literary contracts, and that I as leader should pursue with vigour the task of ordering equipment.

In Great Britain at that time the climate for raising money was against the Expedition and most of the burden fell on George Greenfield. Since we had no intention of announcing the Expedition publicly until we had returned from the training programme in North-West Greenland, our only source of funds was in the form of advances on royalties or payments for the 'first option' on various literary and film copyrights. All the negotiating of these contracts was carried out by George, and his reports at the Committee meetings we held were always listened to with rapt attention. But the bankers on our Committee, not unnaturally, were quite unprepared to recommend a bank loan on the security of literary contracts until the contracts had been signed, and insurance taken out to cover them against failure of the Expedition to get off the ground. As a result, the Expedition had no access to hard cash until a few days before the departure for Greenland of my two companions, Roger Tufft and Allan Gill.

Neither of them were personally involved in the affairs of the Expedition during this period, for Roger was teaching in Cumberland and Allan was in the Arctic. Even Fritz Koerner, the fourth member of the party with whom I had always talked over the problems of the Expedition on my short visits to London, had left the country as part of the 'brain drain' to take up the post of Assistant Professor of Glaciology at Ohio State University.

On my own, from a converted bedroom in my parent's home, I was therefore obliged to operate. The task was not an easy one. Every letter had to be more carefully composed than it might have been had I had the money with which to pay for the equipment or food I was ordering; and in due course I had to relieve the pressure by employing two secretaries and by taking three tranquillizing pills a day. One of these secretaries was based in Lichfield where my home was, the other in London. The Lichfield secretary, a married woman, worked from 1 o'clock until 5 o'clock. My London secretary, Sue Milne, one of Sir Vivian's office staff, worked for me in the evenings or whenever during the day she had a spare moment.

So hectic were the last few weeks before our departure for Greenland that I was driving a hired car a hundred and thirty miles to London every day after having left on tape, or in rough typescript, scores of letters for my Lichfield secretary to work on during the afternoon. I would meet Sue for a beer and a sandwich, give her a list of jobs to do for me and spend the rest of the day rushing all over the City. I would meet Sue again at Sir Vivian's offices about 6 o'clock and together over a pint of beer we would discuss the events of the day, have a working dinner, then work through the evening until about midnight when I would set out to drive back to Lichfield. Often I would fall asleep at the wheel and run into the hard core at the side of the motorway. In due course it became my habit to pull into a service station, curl up on the back seat of the car and snatch a few hours' sleep before continuing the journey in the cold mist of early morning. Arriving back in Lichfield in time for breakfast at 7 a.m., I would work through to ten or eleven and then drive back down to London again.

Crises of one kind or another came thick and fast during those last few weeks. Suppliers would phone up to say they could not meet their deadlines, airline companies would phone to say they could not fit the sledges into the aircraft, and, of course, there were the usual invoices stamped 'final reminder' and other financial embarrassments too painful to recall. The most alarming crisis, however, was when Allan Gill telephoned me from Montreal to say that he had been offered the leadership of the 'Blue Ice' project – an American scientific expedition which was to spend the winter on the Greenland Ice Cap. He had less than a couple of days in which to make up his mind whether or not to take it. Had I been less highly strung as a result of the pressures on me at that time, I would probably have taken all these things in my stride.

Roger I had known for years – we had sailed together on the *Shackleton* way back in 1955. Our first year in Antarctica we had spent on separate bases, but his second and third year we had spent at Hope Bay on the Graham Land Peninsula. We had been in our early twenties then and had no professed ambitions. We were happy enough in the job we were doing and in the sledge journeys we were making. I remembered him as a lean and muscular Welshman as intellectually agile as he was physically impressive – a quiet man with an enormous fund of anecdotes about historical figures. Shortly after he had returned from his spell of three and a half years in the Antarctic, he had joined the crew of Major H. W. Tilman's pilot cutter *Mischief* and sailed with him 21,000 miles visiting the Sub-Antarctic Kerguelen and Crozet Islands. He later sailed 7,000 miles with Tilman in the Arctic, visiting the west coast of Greenland and Baffin Island, made a number of trips to Lapland and spent one summer in Spitzbergen. His most recent trip had been a man-hauling crossing of the Greenland Ice Cap, but several years had passed since I had seen him and inevitably we had changed. He had been excited too many times by plans which had not materialized, and had developed a protective casualness as a defence against disappointments.

Allan and Fritz were very close friends and had both started out their polar careers at Hope Bay in Graham Land. Fritz, with whom I had spent a month right at the end of my first two-and-a-half-year spell, had wintered over at Hope Bay during Roger's third year and had gone on to spend a second winter during which Allan was a member of the party. Between the four of us we had driven dog-teams several thousands of miles.

It did not seem to upset Allan in the least that, having just returned from a spell in the Arctic, he was being driven at eighty miles an hour out to London Airport to catch a flight to 'Ultima Thule'. I was at the wheel. It had been a desperate rush, and so many last-minute snags had occurred that I had been obliged to cancel my flight. The date was the 17th October. Roger and Allan caught the plane, and I went back to work.

The reason why I had chosen the 17th October as the deadline for leaving London was that we had to be at the settlement of Qanaq eighty miles north of Thule, the American strategic airbase, before the 24th October in order that we could erect the hut before the sun set for the last time that year. As for the choice of location – I had wanted to spend the winter with the polar Eskimos. There are very few of them left these days, probably no more than four hundred spread around the five settlements in north-east Greenland. The biggest one, and the administrative centre in the Thule district, is Qanaq. There, from what I could gather from the Ministry for Greenland and the Royal Greenland Trade Department in Copenhagen, were a few Danes, a radio station and a hospital. I knew far more about the settlement of Siorapaluk, for the inhabitants of that settlement had been the subject of a book written in 1955 by a Frenchman, Jean Malaurie. His book, *The Last King of Thule*, was a most readable account of a winter he spent among them, and in my earlier plans I had intended to winter at the same settlement. What finally dissuaded me from doing so was simply a matter of logistics. Siorapaluk is visited by only one ship a year. Unless there is an emergency, no visits are made by the helicopters of the Air Rescue Detachment based at Thule but for a Christmas courtesy call, whereas Qanaq is served by frequent helicopter visits from Thule Air Base throughout the winter – a gesture of goodwill from the Americans much appreciated by the Danes at Qanaq.

All of our heavy equipment, such as the prefabricated hut and the fuel supply, had been sent to Thule earlier in the year from Montreal on the Canadian Coast Guard Icebreaker the *John A. MacDonald*. The remainder of the gear had been divided into two freight loads and sent to Thule via Copenhagen on a charter aircraft of Scandinavian Airlines System. By the kind co-operation of the Americans at Thule, it had been arranged that the entire mass of Expedition equipment would be flown by helicopters of the Air Rescue Detachment to Qanaq, and there, with the permission of the Danish Government, we were to set up our winter quarters.

My thirty-second birthday passed unnoticed, and my new deadline of the 31st October came on at a breathtaking pace. I went everywhere at a frantic speed until my head was spinning, but there were no more Committee Meetings during that period for I was officially away on the Expedition and in every sense living on borrowed time.

My daily drives of two hundred and sixty miles up and down the motorway were nerve-racking affairs, and I often arrived at my destination so tense that I had to shut myself out of sight for half an hour or more until I had regained composure and ceased uncontrollably trembling. From the public telephones at service stations I dictated messages or sent my secretary strings of instructions. I would often pull in and phone my parents to give them a closer estimate of the time I was due in Lichfield, and they would drop every job they were doing in order to lay out in neat array all the gear I needed, or get to work, on my instructions, packing hundreds of awkward-shaped items of Expedition equipment and labelling the boxes.

By Friday, the 18th October, I had transferred my filing cabinet from Lichfield to the Library in Sir Vivian's office, and briefed Sue on the system by which I had kept track of the many thousands of letters the cabinet now contained. That weekend was the most hectic of any in my life, but by Monday morning I was ready and in a daze drove alone to the airport.

I slept all the way to Oslo and on arriving was told over the public address system to go immediately to the Chief Customs Inspector. He warned me to speak to no one but the Deputy Director of the Norsk Polarinstitutt when I passed out of the Customs Hall; and when safely hustled into a car and on my way to town, Kaare Lundquist told me that a young Norwegian by the name of Fløtum, who was himself planning a trans-Arctic journey, had been trying to get an exclusive face-to-face interview with me for which he would be handsomely paid by one of Norway's leading newspapers. Tore Gjelsvik, the Director of the Institute and an old friend of mine, knowing that I was hoping to keep my plans secret until after the successful conclusion of the Greenland training programme, had taken immediate action. He had been one of the leading figures in the Norwegian underground movement during the war. Forestalling Fløtum was to him a relatively simple task; but the incident set me wondering, for Fløtum was only one of many who, if he could raise the money, might succeed in crossing the Arctic Ocean and so claim to have forestalled me. True, Fløtum's proposed route across the Arctic Ocean was by the shorter axis. Indeed, I believe he was then thinking of setting out from Spitzbergen and making for Ellesmere Island via the Pole – a route which subtends an angle of only 95° of longitude. Nevertheless, I recalled uncomfortably the words of Scott on reaching the South Pole and discovering that he had been forestalled by the Norwegian explorer, Amundsen: 'Great God! This is an awful place and terrible enough for us to have laboured to it without the reward of priority.'

I flew on to Copenhagen and from there to Thule, feeling desperately uneasy in spite of Tore Gjelsvik's encouraging remarks that only he who plans a long slow journey stands any chance of success. I had heard too of an American expedition which, during the summer of 1967, was going to make an attempt at the North Pole with Bombardier Skidoos; and a German expedition, also using mechanical vehicles, which planned to set out for the Pole from a base in north-east Greenland. The five million square miles of the Arctic Ocean for the first time seemed too small and the Pole too absurd a goal.

4 Reconnaissance

THE FLIGHT TO GREENLAND WAS UNEVENTFUL IN ONE SENSE, TOO EVENTFUL IN ANOTHER. SO FREQUENTLY WERE WE served with food, we were given no time to sleep, and the Greenland Ice Cap, over which I had first flown in 1960, failed to excite me. I felt washed out. Even when we were forced to make an unscheduled landing at Søndre Strømfjord by a turbulent approach along the fjord, I felt too tired to take an interest. It was along that fjord I had sailed six years before with the dogs which I had collected from the settlements along the west coast – I could see the very spot where I had leapt ashore and tied them up, and the dusty track from the harbour to the airbase. I knew every foot of the way.

The American airbase at Thule proved to be far bigger, its streets far draughtier and the nearby hills more miserable. The sun had set, and at midday Thule was in twilight. The lights of taxis, trucks and heavy plant were pricks of yellow in a blue-grey scene that was raw, cold and very depressing. There was a metal Christmas tree outside the H.Q. – its lights had been switched on ceremonially the day the sun officially set – and recorded bells of a country church played hymn tunes at regular intervals from a rosette of amplifiers on a chapel roof. Men muffled in enormous parkas shuffled from one warm building to another along streets down which ground-drift was snaking past vehicles all plugged with umbilical cords which electrically kept their engines warm. Each building was connected to its neighbour with high-voltage cables and insulated lifelines beneath which the white foxes scampered. The whole camp seemed to be rumbling, and from the vents and chimneys vapour rose or was drawn off by the wind; but in the officers' club, once through the porch and relieved of the heavy fur-hooded parka, one might have been in a select club anywhere in America. There, in a slightly perfumed atmosphere, young officers sat at an elliptical bar drinking apéritifs before going to dinner, or clustered in fours and fives at tables after a meal of King Crab and salad whilst the go-go girls performed.

Every evening for a week I spent the hours of relaxation with the pilots of the air rescue detachment – my days I spent at the base headquarters where my plans were studied with the greatest of interest. The generous help I was offered touched me deeply. Already Roger and Allan, together with some of the fuel and our hut, had been flown to the settlement at Qanaq. My own turn came on the morning of the 10th November. Inspector Orla Sandborg, informally but neatly dressed in a grey shirt and matching grey trousers, had spent most of his life in Greenland. Although still young (he was about thirty-eight), he had held several positions of influence and had the reputation of being a strong but scrupulously fair administrator. He had long since grown out of the idealistic and slightly patronizing attitude which the less experienced Danish administrators have towards the Greenlanders. His was a doctrine influenced by his genuine love of the Eskimos, his subjects, whose language he spoke fluently and whose ways and attitudes he understood.

The Thule District which came under his jurisdiction is a remote one and the last outpost of the polar Eskimos, whose forefathers had come from North America some thousand years ago. Crossing Smith Sound, they had moved down the west coast, around the southern tip, and up along the east coast. Socially cut off from the west-coast Greenlanders by Melville Bay, an area of inclement weather and treacherous icefloes, the Thule Eskimos have in a way become isolated from the changes which have been occurring in the south. They know of these changes, of course, for contrary to the general belief, they are a literate people and newspapers in their own language are eagerly read. They have their own radio programme, too, and there are very few Eskimo homes without a radio set. But even if they had not this news media they would seldom go for more than a year without news from the south, for despite the hazards of Melville Bay there are always a few Thule Eskimos who will make the crossing by dog sledge to visit the Greenland settlements of Upernavik and Umanak. Reports they bring back and the press copy they read tell of a changing way of life where the traditional hunting economy is giving way to a more lucrative fishing industry. In the Thule District, however, the Eskimos are encouraged to hunt, although it would seem they need little persuasion for they are by nature a proud people.

This traditional pride we at first mistook for arrogance. In spite of being well warned by such writers as Peter Freuchen that the Eskimos regard the white men who winter among them as irritable children, we were often irritated by them. Once we had become established in the village, they had visited us on any excuse at all. I cannot really blame them for invading our privacy, for we must have been a source of great amusement to them; indeed, few of them could keep a straight face for more than a few minutes.

The Danes were equally amused but far too discreet to laugh. We had literally landed amongst them without warning. Although Orla Sandborg had known we were coming, his instructions from Copenhagen had been to keep our plans confidential. The crates in which our hut was packed had, like carrion, been carried in slings below the helicopters and in the last grazing rays of the setting sun been gently dropped at the edge of the village. Our red hut, not unlike a tent, had gone up in a hurry, but the small army of Eskimos who had helped to erect it were nowhere to be seen the following day.

The whole set-up to the Danes must have seemed most mysterious. The electrician who had offered to lay electric cables to the hut had been politely told by the two occupants that they preferred to use kerosene lanterns, and rumours spread around the village that the two men were sleeping on packing crates and cooking on primus stoves. They seldom ventured abroad during the day but were occasionally spotted as it got dark, wandering out on the sea ice and along the coast with bundles of rubbish under their arms and bulging from their pockets. In a little while a small fire would be observed a mile away and an hour or two later the men would be seen sneaking back to their huts. The Danes had concluded that Roger and Allan were anti-social since they seldom visited anyone, and were rarely seen in the village store.

I had expected my two colleagues by the time I arrived to have made friends with our neighbours and to have established themselves, but their problems it seems were insuperable. By nature both of them are reserved, and the ordeal of buying provisions at the store from a plump Eskimo girl who shook like a jelly every time she laughed, and laughed every time she looked at them, was evidently disconcerting. Neither of them could summon the courage boldly to ask for each item in English, and their attempts at Danish or at thumbnail sketches had all the Eskimo ladies in stitches. My two companions therefore were ravenous by the time I arrived and bored by their routine, for not until the helicopter flight which brought me in did the bulk of our equipment arrive.

The hut we were testing was essentially a padded tent strapped over a framework of duralumin and heated by a kerosene stove. Cylindrical in shape, the hut had a small porch at one end and a chimney at the other, and at Qanaq was anchored by guy ropes to six sixty-gallon fuel drums. The floor dimensions were 16 feet by 12 feet – hardly enough room in which to swing a cat by the time we got ourselves organized inside with three camp-beds and a cooking-table. If the hut worked out satisfactorily, I planned to dismantle it and ship it to Resolute Bay after we had finished with it at Qanaq. It would later be airdropped to us and serve as our winter quarters during our drift across the Pole. The same general policy applied to all our other items of gear – everything was to be tested first, modified if necessary, and used again during the trans-Arctic journey. After a few days, I had decided on our first modification. Our dwelling would have to be enlarged to 16 feet by 16 feet for the winter drift on the Arctic Ocean. The extra section I immediately ordered, and arranged to have sent to Resolute Bay, our main staging depot for the supplies we would require during the trans-Arctic journey.

We set up beds and a cooking-table, at one end of which I allocated myself space for an office. We built shelves for the food and our small library of books, and pitched a tent outside in which to store experimental food which had been donated by the U.S. Army Natick Laboratories. Around the walls we hung our ropes and gear and in no time at all the hut had taken on the appearance of an expedition base. By thus exposing our goods and chattels, however, we laid ourselves open to criticism. Some of the Danes thought it was some form of 'expensive joke', but the Eskimos in their criticism were more robust and with macabre delight marked the map on the door (which showed our proposed sledging route from Qanaq to Resolute Bay) with crosses where they predicted the expedition would perish.

Had they not already formed their opinion, they must surely, by the time we started buying their dogs, have thought we were incompetent. For several weeks from the ribs of our hut hung carcasses of seal; in order to feed our dogs we had first to thaw out the frozen seals before we could gut them and chop them up. The floor became so greasy with blubber and blood that it was practically impossible to keep a footing. We had been accustomed in the Antarctic to doing everything ourselves; we felt it would be admitting failure to enlist the help of the

Eskimos; but our problems in Greenland were different from those we had met in the South. At Qanaq we were living in a community of two hundred Eskimos and twenty-five Danes – very different from a community of twelve men in isolation where there were no social strata and no need to dress for dinner. We had come to Greenland prepared for a polar expedition and had found, much to our embarrassment, that we were frequently invited to parties at which the Danes formally and courteously entertained one another. We felt unclean in their presence no matter how much we scrubbed, and yet felt over-dressed in the presence of the Eskimos with whom we had hoped to spend the winter. Reluctantly we accepted our situation and altered our routine.

We took over a small hut offered us by the Greenland Technical Organization and in this we stored our supply of seal and walrus carcasses. By that time the object of our sojourn had become common knowledge in the Thule District, and among the Danes and the Eskimos we had made many friends. Not all of them we knew by name, and for our convenience (and of course in private) we used such nicknames as 'Warm inner-glow', 'Mrs Cut-purse', and 'Little worried frown'. The walrus carcasses, for a small charge, were thawed out and cut up in the home of 'Limpy', one of our Eskimo neighbours, and every second day we collected and fed four pounds of warm meat to each of our twenty dogs. The dogs' harnesses were made up for us by 'Mr Okee-dokee', another of our Eskimo neighbours, and our rubbish collected and water delivered in milk churns by 'Nut' and his friend 'Crackers'. Electricity was laid on and we were given a key to the shower over at the power-house. After a month or so, when the Eskimos had mellowed enough to give us some of the advice which was the prime purpose of our sojourn in Greenland and the sledging journey which was to follow, they would for hours sit in our hut and with crude diagrams and drawings show us how they hunted seal during the winter night. They shook their heads sadly, however, when they saw us assemble our two sledges. One was an exact replica of a sledge which had survived Peary's last journey over the polar pack ice; the other was modelled on one used by Steffanson during his long journeys on to the polar pack between 1914 and 1918. Each sledge was about twenty inches wide – too narrow for the heavy loads we would be carrying, the Eskimos said. They predicted that neither sledge would survive the journey to Resolute Bay and urged us to use three-foot-wide Eskimo sledges instead. We found it unthinkable to exchange our two beautifully constructed English-made sledges for the crude Eskimo counterparts, but both our sledges were to shatter before we had travelled further than forty miles from Qanaq. We finished the preliminary trip with Eskimo sledges – and the sledges we were to use on the trans-Arctic journey were wider ones, made according to the Eskimo recommendations.

Another Eskimo suggestion we were to adopt was the use of fur clothing. Furs had not been used on Antarctic expeditions for over fifty years, because they aren't really necessary. The Antarctic explorer seldom requires clothing as warm as this since he rarely travels in temperatures below minus 50° Fahrenheit and in such temperatures lightweight windproof anoraks worn over woollen clothing are generally adequate. In Greenland, so we were told, caribou parkas and polar bear pants were essential, so we were duly measured and fitted out. During the next few months, however, the caribou parkas shed their hair – there is an old saying in the Arctic that you are not an explorer until you have eaten your own weight in caribou hair – so, having qualified by this definition and learned our lesson, the furs we eventually adopted for use on the trans-Arctic journey were wolfskin, carefully tanned and expertly made up for us by a fur trader in Fairbanks, Alaska.

Both our sledges and our furs we tried out during the winter night on sledging journeys to the neighbouring Greenland villages, and by the New Year 1967, the two teams of dogs we had bought were settling down. It was on one of these runs that Roger and Allan met Cali Peary, the son of the American explorer Robert E. Peary, and father of Peter who was to be one of our guides up the coast of Greenland and across Smith Sound to Canada.

There are lots of stories about Cali Peary and some of them no doubt are true. He is reputed to be very rich, and on one occasion to have written to the President of the United States claiming that, as the son of a famous American explorer, he ought to be paid a pension. He is reported also to be the only Eskimo who forcibly restrained a representative of the Greenland administration from painting a number on his house.

The Eskimo son of Peary's Negro servant, Mathew Henson, also lives in the Thule District and, although there are no Eskimo offspring of Dr Frederick Cook, the brother and children of Etukishook, one of Cook's two Eskimo companions, often came to visit us. It would have been fascinating, had we been able to speak their language, to have discussed details of the stories told them by that famous old hunter, for in spite of the language barrier we were able to gather from gestures and rude noises that they considered Cook a faker. Most of the Eskimos with whom we discussed Cook's claims believe that the doctor and his two Eskimo companions, after having crossed Ellesmere Island, went south-west instead of north-west; and instead of sledging up Nansen Sound to the northern tip of Axel Heiberg Island from where he set out across the polar pack ice towards the North Pole, spent the summer of 1908 hunting in the region of Hell Gate off the south-east coast of Ellesmere Island. The Eskimos are excellent map-readers – we could see this from the way they ran their grubby fingers over the map on the inner door of our hut as they vividly described some hunting anecdote, or traced the route we planned on taking, up to the point where they predicted we would perish. They must have known Cook and his Eskimo companions had sledged north-west – the stories handed down over the years could not have been so far distorted. We can only assume, therefore, that the Eskimos told us (as their fathers had told Peary and MacMillen) what they thought we wanted to hear.

With the route we ourselves proposed taking and with the techniques we intended using, there was much more honest criticism from the Eskimos, and some straight talking from Orla Sandborg too. It was, he felt, his responsibility to see us safely out of his territory. The U.S. Air Force at Thule airbase felt a similar responsibility for our safety, and although both Orla and the U.S.A.F. had confidence in us, I have no doubt they breathed a sigh of relief when, from Alexandra Fjord (an abandoned Royal Canadian Mounted Police post on the west side of Smith Sound), I was able to get a radio message out saying that all was well.

The final weeks before our departure from Qanaq had been every bit as hectic as the period immediately prior to our departure from London. We had by that time become familiar figures around the village, and many of the prestige Eskimos had developed the habit of dropping in to see us. This was all most encouraging, for with their friendship and (provided that we completed the journey) a small measure of respect, we stood a far better chance of persuading them to provide us with dogs for the trans-Arctic trek. We had also by that time become socially acceptable with the Danish community at Qanaq and the personal friends of Orla Sandborg, without whose help we would have found it extremely difficult to carry out our programme.

It was through Orla that we were to be introduced to Kissunguak, a well-built, cheerful but superior Eskimo who accepted more as an obligation than a pleasure the task of guiding us safely out of the Thule District and across Smith Sound to Canada. His reputation as a dog handler and a hunter was supreme, and he was very ambitious. One day, he would represent the Thule District in the Greenland Council for 'his

dogs are lions and his wife is a goddess'. Several times I invited
him to visit our hut but he had neither the time nor the
inclination until early in the New Year when, with Peter Peary
and Peter's wife, he came to look us over. He had by then
decided to stand for election to the Greenland Council, and he
had nominated Peter to take his place on the trip to Canada.

With this arrangement we were delighted, for Peter was
already familiar with the ways and strange ambitions of
explorers. He had accompanied the Norwegian Bjørn Staib
as far as Alert, the point from where Staib had launched his
attempt at a trans-Arctic crossing in 1964. That Norwegian
assault, which had been sponsored by the National Geographic
Society, had aimed at crossing the Arctic Ocean in one head-
long dash. It was an expedition which had failed not through
lack of courage or lack of financial support (as far as I can
gather), but because the start was made too late in the season
from a point on the edge of the Arctic Ocean where there was
a tremendous build-up of pressure. By good fortune, the
American scientific drifting station, Arlis 2 (which has long
since drifted out of the Arctic Ocean and melted), was at that
time drifting across Staib's route about halfway from Greenland to the North Pole. He located it and from there was flown
out. Peter Peary's part in that 'sporting challenge' had been to
build Eskimo sledges to replace those of Staib's which had
broken up in the first few miles of the journey – and Peter was
to witness the break up of more sledges before his career was
much older.

Peter and his wife, Imanguak, were delightfully relaxed and
had not – or, at least, concealed – any doubts that we would be
ready to start on the 26th February. Much more characteristic
of the Eskimo in features, build and temperament was Kaunguak and his woman, Nivikinguak, who were to join us at
Siorapaluk, a village two days journey to our west. It had been
arranged through Orla Sandborg that the four of them would
accompany us as far as Alexandra Fjord on the west side of

Smith Sound; they were to be our guides and hunters and were to carry on their sledges some of our provisions. For their help we were to pay Peter and Kaunguak ninety dollars each – a not unreasonable sum considering that they were going to cross Smith Sound anyway on their annual polar bear hunt. But the spring hunting trip is the one time of the year when Eskimos become impatient, and Kaunguak was no exception.

The date I had originally set for our departure from Qanaq was the 8th February, ten days before sunrise in that latitude; but we had to set back our start a couple of weeks in order that we could film the rituals and orgies we assumed would mark the end of the winter night. It was very disappointing. We saw not one Eskimo leaping in the air as the sun climbed over the southern horizon for the first time in four months, and to the best of our knowledge not a single Eskimo lost more sleep that Saturday than he usually did.

We started dismantling the hut in earnest about 2.00 p.m. on the 25th February and had it flat on the ground in less than two hours. There was no lack of assistance or of scavengers, and there were a good number of sightseers too; but by 7.00 p.m. the Eskimos had all gone home to their little wooden huts.

Early the following morning they turned out again. To see three 'kraslunas' dressed up like Eskimos in their polar bear pants and 'kamiks' and enormous parkas made of reindeer skin was an occasion not to be missed. Trying hard to be inconspicuous, we moved out on to the sea ice with our two sledges loaded with nine hundred pounds of gear on each. We had cameras, tape-recorders, radio transmitters, dog food, man rations, a large quantity of fuel – for we were expecting temperatures well below minus 50° Fahrenheit during the crossing of Ellesmere Island – camping gear, and a variety of clothing so comprehensive that we were equipped for any climatic condition likely to be met north of the tropic of Cancer. Seldom had we ever before set out on a sledging journey with such enormous loads. In addition to what we carried on the sledges, a sizable amount of gear belonging to us was being hauled by Peter Peary's superb team of dogs. We had little or no alternative. The journey ahead of 1,500 miles was a long one by any standards, and there were only two places along our proposed route where we could collect a prearranged supply of provisions. We were committing ourselves to a journey tougher than any we had previously experienced, a journey from which there could be no turning back without shame and financial embarrassments too disgraceful to consider.

The relief when once we were on our way was almost unbelievable, and as the sledges moved westwards, the winter through which we had just passed seemed like a busy dream, a pantomime of colourful characters in situations too absurd to have been taken seriously. It was several hours before I realized I was feeling cold and miserable. The creaking sledge was so soothing a sound and the surface of the sea ice so smooth that I slipped into a day dream from which I did not awaken until the leading sledge turned into the coast and stopped.

At a small refuge hut we spent the night. The following morning we set off for Siorapaluk. The journey was an easy one, the weather not too windy, and we reached the village feeling very hungry – but were given nothing to eat. Everyone was friendly enough, but we were given nothing the following morning either, and had I not been awakened early by the pangs of hunger and watched our hosts closely as they pottered about the hut, I would have sworn that they were secretly snatching a bite when they thought I was not watching. But they ate nothing all that day, and when at last evening came and they warmed up some seal meat, there was hardly enough of it to feed one healthy adult let alone a hut full of inquisitive Eskimos and three ravenous Europeans.

That first day in Siorapaluk we had spent in checking our gear and dividing it into three loads. Even on the short journey from Qanaq it had become evident that our sledges were not wide enough to take the massive loads and I had decided to buy a third, an Eskimo sledge, which would relieve them of some of the weight. We had set out from Qanaq with twenty-two dogs – I bought another three at fifteen dollars each.

On the morning of the 1st March, Roger, Peter and Imanguak set off ahead of Allan and myself with the arrangement that we would meet them further up the coast at a nest of three huts called Neki. Allan and I covered the preparations and the start of their journey with two movie cameras, and spent the rest of the day making ready the third sledge. By lunch-time half the village was tipsy.

I had seen drunken Eskimos three times before – on the 1st December, 1st January and 1st February. On a points rationing system the inhabitants of the Thule District (Danish administrators and British Expeditions included) are allowed per person one bottle of spirits, two bottles of wine or twenty small bottles of beer a month. The Eskimos invariably buy a bottle of whisky and finish it off in one lurching tour of the village. At Qanaq our hut had been bypassed by most of the Eskimos, consequently we had not become involved in the orgies on the first of each month; but at Siorapaluk, Allan and I were right in the thick of it and the focal point of interest.

With the exception of Inutasuak, an old hunter of great dignity who had travelled in his youth with Edward Shackleton (now Lord Shackleton, Leader of the House of Lords), every Eskimo in the village was rotten by nine o'clock. Men were squaring up to each other and then falling over, old crones were screaming like stuck pigs or sobbing, and wide-eyed children were cowering in the corners or hiding beneath thin blankets on sleeping-platforms on which their elders were wrestling in a stupor of fornication. From each hut in the village came the roars of lunatics and the thud of falling bodies. Doors were wrenched open and, framed for a moment in the light of a lantern, bow-legged drunks lurched out into the night.

Through the village at midnight I followed the old man. He was in a hurry, and the thin shaft of light from his torch did not

73

for one moment change its angle, nor did he once look up. He was disgusted with his fellow villagers and ashamed that I had witnessed the 'Inouit' (the man *par excellence*) in their weakness. 'Drink and the Eskimos no good – no good, NO GOOD,' he kept saying. Inutasuak had admired Edward Shackleton's determination and enjoyed his company, and in a little hut set apart from the village – a hut so drifted in with snow that I had stumbled into the tunnel leading to the door before I had realized we were there – he showed me his treasured possessions: an autographed copy of *South*, the story of Sir Ernest Shackleton's *Endurance* expedition, and many snapshots taken during his journeys with Shackleton's son.

He told me too of the Sverdrup Pass, and his sketch-maps confirmed Dr Cook's account of a long easy climb from the head of Flagler Bay along a frozen river-bed. I would, he told me, have to make a detour to the north after I had passed a watershed, for a glacier blocks the river valley which descends into Irene Bay. This same glacier had been mentioned by both Sverdrup and Cook, but by none of the Eskimos we had met at Qanaq – why, I do not know.

We got away to a late start the following day. Kaunguak and his woman, Nivikinguak, set off first, followed by Thomas and Maktok Kiviok, and the cousin of Peter Peary. Allan and I, each with a sledge, were last of the line – six sledges in all – and within a quarter of an hour they were out of sight and we were creeping along on our own. The three Eskimos who had joined us were also going across Smith Sound after polar bears.

By nightfall we were still four miles from the huts at Neki, on ice only a few inches thick and so black that it was like a sea of ink. The sledges slid over it without the slightest vibration, and had we not spotted the torchlights of our Eskimo friends when we were still two miles from the huts, we would probably have had to feel our way along the coast until we literally stumbled upon them. It was a memorable ride and a cheerful reunion when at last we reached the rough ice of the coast where six teams of dogs were tethered and eight cheerful fur-clad figures were busy chopping up walrus to feed them.

The following morning, for the first time since leaving Qanaq six days before, we set off with our full party plus three travelling companions – a total of eight sledges. We made good progress across the first bay, but at the second point the sea ice was not strong enough to bear our weight, and farther on we could see open water. We had no alternative but to clamber over the pressure ice and up on to the coastal piedmont. Here the sledging was not easy, for the snow-covered ledge was sloping towards the sea, and the sledges were constantly side-slipping. Several times the sledges rolled over or crashed against boulders, and at one point the ledge was only two feet six inches wide. This was a difficult place to get past with the Eskimo sledges which were three feet or more in width. On one side of the ledge was an overhanging rock – on the other side a drop of twenty feet to the sea which was beating a fine cold spray over the ice-cliffs.

It was in a situation such as this that the Eskimos excelled. The technique of negotiating the obstacle was simple enough, and had we not been accompanied by Eskimos we would have got round it in the same way. Where the Eskimos differed from us was in their attitude to the problem: they took it all in their stride and evidently enjoyed the whole operation of roping up the sledges one at a time and manhandling them, still fairly fully loaded, across that precarious ledge. We were to learn a great deal from the Eskimos during the next few weeks which would stand us in good stead, not only during the journey ahead but in the more arduous and protracted journey we were to make across the Arctic Ocean. Some of these lessons were simply tips on technique – more important by far was the impression they made on us as people. They do not, as do most Europeans, regard the Arctic as a hostile environment – rather a setting in which to test themselves. To the Arctic they are perfectly attuned and are seldom, if ever, in a hurry.

Nevertheless, the rough sledging along the ledge took its toll. Our sledges rolled over from time to time and crashed into boulders, and the Steffanson sledge was smashed beyond repair. Then our Eskimo sledge was badly damaged. There was nothing we could do but return to Siorapaluk to replace them. Allan and I raced back for two more sledges and five more dogs, and then retraced our tracks along the coast, adding one hundred miles to our trip.

Kaunguak and Nivikinguak had awaited our arrival while the others in the party had continued up the coast. It was to be four days before we caught up with them at Etah, an abandoned Eskimo village. Much of the trip to Etah we had to make over an inland route because of open water along the coast, and a very tough journey it proved to be. On several occasions, we had to hitch all of our dogs to a single sledge in order to haul it up the ice falls and across stretches of bare rock. Many of the descents we made in pitch darkness were terrifying, but the techniques of sledging we picked up from the Eskimos were later to prove invaluable.

From Etah our united party journeyed up the Greenland coast to about latitude 78°34′ N where we came upon an ice bridge spanning the entire thirty-five miles across Smith Sound. The ice bridge was a narrow frozen oasis in a liquid desert about four miles wide at its widest point – the most chaotic ice pack I have ever seen. Fortunately, however, there was a strip of smooth ice on the southern edge, a strip in places no more than a few hundred yards wide, which provided good smooth sledging right the way across to Canada. Only once in the last twenty years has the ice in that strait not held during the months of February, March and April. Every year except one it has provided the Polar Eskimos from the Thule District with an ice bridge to their hunting territories on the east coast of Ellesmere Island. In fact, so traditional has become this route that the Royal Canadian Mounted Police set up a station in Alexandra Fjord to intercept the Greenland Eskimos on their way across, and drive them back to Greenland; for the polar bears that freely roam along the east coast of Ellesmere Island are regarded by the R.C.M.P. as the preserve of the Canadian Eskimos, the cousins of the Thule people. Our travelling companions were obviously in great fear of the R.C.M.P. and illustrated their stories of encounters with the Mounties with outrageous exaggeration. Imagine their delight when, on the Greenland side of the ice bridge on a day that was dead calm and cold, we saw against a back-drop of blue-grey clouds three blurred and distorted yellow forms miraged above the horizon moving in slow procession south across our path. Without a word louder than a whisper, five sledges were hastily unloaded and in less than a minute were skidding away from us after the bears. They were the first polar bears I had seen in their wild, free state. We were to see many more over the next few years and at far closer quarters. We were also, in time, to come to regard them as a menace. But on that day in Smith Sound they looked too magnificent as they shuffled across the skyline to be anything less than a manifestation of some kind of god in triplicate.

We reached the now deserted R.C.M.P. post at Alexandra fjord on the afternoon of the 18th March. We had come about two hundred and fifty miles from Qanaq, and three of our Eskimo friends had already left us. Peary and Kaunguak urged us once again to change our plans and not take the route across Ellesmere Island by the Sverdrup Pass – a river bed that had brought Cook from the inland end of Flagler Bay without difficulty to the other side of the island. Inutasuak, the old hunter we had met at Siorapaluk, had confirmed Cook's report that this was a long easy climb, and had cautioned us that we would have to make one detour north in order to bypass the glacier that blocks a portion of the river valley. Peary and Kaunguak had warned us that if there was little snow in the valley we would run into trouble, and had suggested that we go over an ice cap to the south of the pass – a far surer way of crossing the island, and the way the island was usually crossed by the R.C.M.P. and the Eskimos.

One by one on the morning of the 21st, our four companions had poked their heads through the sleeve entrance of our tent to say goodbye. Peter had been first as usual – a more energetic Eskimo I had never met. He had inherited more from his illustrious grandfather than his famous name. He had attributes of leadership uncommon among the Eskimos, and a lively interest in the outside world; a lively sense of humour too. Often, throwing some article of clothing on the floor, he would order his wife to pick it up, then, as she did so, roar with laughter. He had the gait of a polar Eskimo – a bow-legged lurch, but his facial features were European enough. I would not go so far as to say that one could mistake him for an Englishman in the foyer of Claridges; but the carpets of Claridges are probably the last soft surface on earth he would wish to tread, for he is a hunter, one of the finest of the Thule District, and his wife, Imanguak, one of the most attractive, full-blooded and moody women of the North.

Even as Peter shook hands with the three of us, we had sensed the urgency of the hunter's pulse. It had been in the firm handshake of his wife too. I can see her now; dressed in polar bear pants, and a flimsy blue anorak – and Kaunguak, his full brown face split with a grin not quite sincere, for we were to him, even after sharing so many adventures, still the 'kraslunas', the men from the south, inferior to the 'Inouit', the 'real men', the Eskimaux. He had been annoyed with his woman, Nivikinguak, whose eyes were full of tears. She was the only one showing emotion, the only one genuinely sad at the moment of parting.

We had been travelling with the Eskimos for about a month. We had grown to trust and respect them, and felt miserable as we watched those two sledges gliding off into the mist. Ahead lay a journey of over a thousand miles – a journey which was itself merely a training trip for the more arduous trans-polar trek that had been several years in the planning.

At the head of Flagler Bay, the island was about fifty miles wide. Cook, according to his account, made the crossing in four days. It took us almost four weeks.

By the 6th April we had only nine days food left for ourselves and nine days food for the dogs, providing we were prepared to kill three of them. Roger considered we should kill five, and Allan was of the opinion we ought to jettison all unessential gear, such as the Bell & Howell movie camera and the reserve radio. He wanted to cut the end off his sledge to lighten it, and ditch his furs now that the weather was becoming a little warmer; but on further discussion we agreed that the saving in weight would not appreciably alter our situation. We were suffering, we thought, from the accumulated effects of carbon monoxide poisoning – all the symptoms were there – the dizziness, the nausea, the sensation of drunkenness, the debilitating lethargy. It didn't help much being on only one-quarter of our normal ration, nor would the situation have been half as serious if the dogs had been in good condition. But they were even hungrier than ourselves, and as confused as we were frustrated by all the bare ground. Had we taken the advice of the Eskimos and attempted the crossing of Ellesmere Island by way of the ice-cap, we would have been at Eureka station by that time. As it was, we were only half-way across the Sverdrup Pass with all the difficult parts of the route still ahead.

It had been fifteen days since we had left the Eskimos, but it had seemed more like five weeks since that emotional parting. It was the low point in the journey and there was talk of radioing ahead for help and giving up. But the prospect was unthinkable. It was obvious that Cook, and a handful of other explorers who had managed to cross this Sverdrup Pass, had found far more snow and passable sledging than we had, but that would be small excuse to sponsors who knew only that Ellesmere had been crossed before and that we had failed. I recognized that if we stopped now, we could forget our dream of crossing the Arctic Ocean.

We killed one dog and fed him to the others, and from that day on slept outside and only used the tent as a shelter in which to cook our meals. We entered a canyon which in places was not wide enough to take a sledge. Every item of gear had to be back-packed through this canyon and the sledge manhandled, twisted and turned, and in some places lowered down frozen waterfalls. We reached the end of the canyon which opened out into a frozen lake; it was blocked at the western end by the glacier tongue about which we had been warned by the Eskimos, and in the accounts of the crossing of Ellesmere by Sverdrup and Cook. Every item of gear was back-packed around the edge of the glacier tongue; beyond, on a river of blue ice, we made slightly better progress down towards Irene Bay.

We were now down to one sixth of our normal daily ration and were further weakened by the after-effects of the insidious carbon monoxide poisoning. We had, in crossing Ellesmere Island, covered at least three times the shortest distance from one side of the island to the other. We staggered on to the fjord, gaunt and weary. Even on the most perfect sea ice we could seldom get the dogs to haul the sledges faster than two miles in an hour; and at times, pulling the sledge with one hand, we could overtake them. We had planned no air drops of supplies – as we had for the projected Arctic crossing – on this training trip. Moreover, with the warm weather and the break-up of the ice drawing near, we could not afford to lose time by going off hunting in the hope of getting food for the dogs or for ourselves. Ironically, however, we did receive some help by air – though it did not do the dogs much good. The first of our scheduled supply points was a Canadian station at Eureka, located about half way up the coast of Ellesmere Island, somewhere about one hundred and fifty miles north-west from where we were in Bay Fjord. Concerned because we were so long overdue, the station had radioed us that an aeroplane was on its way. Eureka at that time was also serving as headquarters for an unusual venture led by Ralph Plaisted and backed by the Columbia Broadcasting System. His idea was to try and reach the North Pole from Eureka, a distance of about seven hundred miles, using motorized sledges (Bombadier Skidoos). The expedition had faltered within days of setting out, and by the time we reached Eureka had well and truly failed. But at that time the Plaisted expedition was still in fairly good heart, and it was Plaisted's support aircraft that was now on its way to pick us up. I visualized banner headlines in the world press announcing that our expedition had been rescued by Plaisted's expedition, and over the radio asked Plaisted to kindly return to his base. By then, however, the plane was overhead and had spotted us. It was equipped with skis, and came down and landed. After emphasizing that we had no intention of abandoning our trip, and after being assured by Plaisted that the gesture was made in good faith, we accepted some provisions and a metal sledge to replace the Peary-type sledge which Roger had been obliged to abandon half-way across Ellesmere Island.

Over the next few days we drove ourselves hard, and on the 26th April, exactly two months since leaving the Eskimo settlement at Qanaq, we sighted the fourteen-man weather station Eureka in the distance.

In such poor shape were we and the dogs on approaching Eureka that one dog collapsed and died within a mile of the station, while we, exhausted and emaciated, were obliged to gorge and rest ourselves for a week before we could move on.

On the 6th May, the day after Plaisted's plan had been officially abandoned, we set out from Eureka station on the second half of our journey. Ahead of us was seven hundred miles of ice which would get weaker by the day.

We touched the northern tip of Axel Heiberg Island, well above eighty-one degrees north latitude, on the evening of 11th May, and stood in wonder at the spot Dr Cook had claimed had been the jumping-off place for his assault on the North

Pole. The view seemed uncommonly barren. Not a sign of wild life or movement could be seen, and all around us was the forbidding bleakness of ice and snow.

We now started down the other side of Axel Heiberg Island and began our southward journey. Once past the polar pack ice, the going became a little smoother; but our dogs were tiring again, and the sight of Meighen Island, after sledging for about one hundred and twenty miles, was a relief. On this remote and uninhabited island our final supply depot had been laid on the ice cap at an altitude of about one thousand feet by an aircraft of the Polar Continental Shelf Project.

We climbed wearily up to the ice cap, quickly loaded our supplies and left early on the morning of the 22nd May. Time was now of pressing concern. Spring had come to the region to the south, and the ice would soon be breaking up around us. We had approximately four hundred miles to go to reach Resolute Bay, and there wasn't a moment to spare. In our favour was the fact that we now had continual daylight, but as we raced over the smooth ice southwards we ran into heavy fog. For several days the sun was barely visible. There were no tide cracks around the islands we could follow, and being only a few hundred miles from the North Magnetic Pole our compasses were unreliable. Eventually the blizzards came and for ten days, in visibility of less than ten yards, we had to lie up and wait. It was an anxious period. There was no way of knowing if the ice around us was cracking up. We dared not head due south for the northern tip of Devon Island for fear of running into trouble.

When we were eventually able to move, we had to cover miles and cover them fast. I estimated we had to average a minimum of twenty miles each day. The dogs, hungry again, were not up to it. We could barely travel faster than one mile per hour. As a result, we had to sledge fifteen or sixteen hours each day to make our daily distances, travelling for eight, resting the dogs for four, and then sledging for another eight hours.

By forced marches we reached Arthur Fjord on Devon Island on the 16th June. There we got the news we had feared: the ice in the channel north-east of Resolute had broken up. Our trip was over, just one hundred miles short of the goal.

It was most disappointing later to discover that the pilots who had passed this information had been mistaken. The ice in places was still firm enough for us to have sledged right through to Resolute Bay. On the other hand, the ice over which we had been travelling during the past few days was swept away only a week or so later, so on the balance I think we were fairly lucky and came out well ahead.

I was picked up and flown with some of the dogs to Resolute Bay. Allan, Roger, and the remainder of the dogs and gear, reached Resolute a week later. Arrangements were made through the Royal Canadian Mounted Police for our dogs to be shipped to the Eskimo settlement in Jones Sound. The remainder of the stores and equipment was left at Resolute Bay and would be air-dropped to us later, during the crossing of the Arctic Ocean.

We then went our separate ways. Roger caught a plane to Edmonton, and from there on to Montreal, where he planned to have a short holiday before returning home. Allan, true to form, had committed himself to another expedition. Within minutes of arriving at Resolute Bay, he was taking off again to fly to the base camp on Devon Island where, for the remainder of the summer, he would be station leader of the Arctic Institute of North America's Expedition. He was to join me in England in the autumn to help with the massive paperwork and final planning of the Arctic crossing. I flew to Edmonton, and from there directly to London.

5 Last-Minute Rush

WEARING A SUNBLEACHED SHAGGY BEARD WHICH I HAD
HAD NO TIME TO TRIM, A PAIR OF KHAKI SLACKS AND A
fawn-coloured anorak, I arrived at London airport on 30 June
1967, sun-tanned and more fit than I had felt in many years.
I hired a car and drove to the warehouse of my freight
agents and checked through Customs two hunting-rifles,
two revolvers, £800 worth of camera equipment and a few
items of personal gear; bundled it all into the boot of the
car and drove directly to Red Lion Square to see George
Greenfield.

It was a business meeting as exciting as any I can remember,
for my friend and literary agent for perhaps the first time in
our long association could see light at the far end of the tunnel.
He laid out for me an itinerary covering my first few days in
U.K. and urged me to seek a meeting of the Committee of
Management at the earliest opportunity to work out a plan of
campaign. To say I was eager to begin would be an understatement; I was as impatient to plunge in at the deep end as a
man on fire, and had George not counselled me from his long
experience of expeditioning, it would not have occurred to me
that my first priority was to get a haircut and the second, to
buy an outfit more appropriate to the City.

It was a Friday. I was to go into hiding for the weekend
and drive to a rendezvous with three representatives of *The
Sunday Times* at an inn a few miles from Reading the following
Monday, when I would be interviewed about my past and
grilled about my proposed trans-Arctic journey. I left George

and the following morning drove hard to Cambridge, had lunch with Sir Vivian and Lady Fuchs and drove on even harder to Lichfield where, impatiently, I paced around the garden of my parents' home and from one pub to another until Monday; then, with a sense of release, I roared down the motorway to my 'secret' meeting with *The Sunday Times*. By Tuesday morning I felt drained of every memory I had stored over the last thirty-odd years, for I had been interrogated into confessing every half-formed ambition and attitude of mind that I subconsciously possessed. The result was a half-page spread in *The Sunday Times* on the 9th July in which under the title *The Longest, Loneliest Walk in the World* Peter Dunn had presented my plan. *The Times* followed this up on Monday with a front-page article but the proposed British Trans-Arctic Expedition was ignored by every other national newspaper.

Eleven days after my return to London, well-scrubbed and more neatly dressed, I reported to the Committee of Management at a meeting held in Sir Vivian's office. The usefulness of the Greenland training programme I assessed in terms of lessons learnt, and listed the items of gear which would have to be modified or replaced. But the bankers were worried men. Mr Tritton reminded us that, although the literary contracts negotiated by Mr Greenfield could expect to yield £48,000, £8,000 of this had already been received of which £7,000 had already been spent. I needed an imprest account, an office, a secretary, a car and an interest-free bridging loan of £50,000, but the financial climate in Britain at that time was not very healthy. The banks were being squeezed hard and the rich men were all surrounded by their private armies with instructions to keep at bay all young beggars with bright ideas. Nor, the Chairman explained, could there be any question of seeking Royal Patronage until the financial situation of the Expedition became a little clearer.

To add to our problems I was committed to producing a

15,000-word article for *True* magazine in America by the end of August, and a book of 100,000 words on my Antarctic experiences, *A World of Men*, for Eyre and Spottiswoode by December. The quality of the film we had shot during the Greenland training programme was unsatisfactory, and the B.B.C. were considering withdrawing from the negotiations for coverage of the trans-Arctic journey. We were informed by the Royal Geographical Society that their support of the Expedition covered only the Greenland training programme, and that I would have to submit yet another proposal and present myself yet again for questioning. Thus blinded by excitement, I had run into my first obstacles, few of which could be completely ignored for the simple reason that they would tend, if ignored, to recur. As for the solutions, we generally used one of three methods: diplomacy, sound business practice or the fast flamboyant approach. I understood only the last.

Within three days of the first committee meeting, I had acquired an office, a secretary and a car. The office was a beautiful room in the Royal Geographical Society which housed the polar books, and which had until a few days before been the office of Mr Crone, the historian and chief librarian; my new secretary was Miss Frankie Ryan, whom I had selected from among some twenty-five applicants because she was not only the most attractive but was, as I discovered over a couple of pints of beer, temperamentally the most compatible; the car I had seen in a display window at 9.00 a.m. and bought by 11.00 a.m. the same day on a borrowed down payment of £200 and several further commitments of £88 per month. Neither the method of choosing a secretary nor the spontaneous purchase of a car could be regarded as sound business practice, but since what I required of the former was a vivacious and compelling female capable of disarming opposition, and what I required of the vehicle was immediate mobility and speed, the action in each case therefore to me at least made sense.

The proposed journey across the Arctic Ocean was regarded by our sponsors as a fine feat but also a financial gamble; it was regarded by me as an exciting pioneer journey that could not be launched if there was any hesitation or delay in ordering equipment, any penny-pinching or any relaxation on my part of the high-pressured single-mindeness of purpose. I considered the function of the Committee was to guide, counsel, encourage, and temper my enthusiasm; to use their far-ranging influence in the City to ease my workload, and to check at our fortnightly meetings the progress of a project which I had on my own been planning for four years and was now, against the clock, erecting on the foundation of their wide and varied experience.

During the nine months I had been away in Greenland, Squadron Leader Freddie Church of the Royal Air Force had attended several meetings of the Committee as an adviser on radio communications. I had first met him at the Ministry of Technology which I had visited for advice on what type of radio equipment I should take on the trans-Arctic journey. I remember very well the first words exchanged between us: he had sat listening intently, as I expounded the plan to a small gathering of technical experts in a room full of grey filing-cabinets and inexpensive furniture. Even before I had finished Freddie had chipped in and expressed himself keen to join in the Expedition – 'You're too bloody old,' I had said jokingly, giving it no more thought. Evidently Freddie did not share my view, and in preparing his brilliant communications plan had in effect written himself into the scheme as a radio relay operator who would be stationed initially at Barrow, Alaska, the starting-point of the crossing; transfer his station at the appropriate stage to the American scientific drifting camp T-3 on the Arctic Ocean and finally to Spitzbergen, with the object of keeping at all times within 500 miles of the crossing party. He did so, of course, not without embarrassment in view of the comment I had made several months before and was at pains to point out on my return—that the whole idea was subject to my approval.

Freddie was thus seconded to the Expedition for its duration by the Ministry of Defence, and a man more devoted to his job or more loyal to his colleagues I have never met. For sixteen months he was the Expedition's link with the outside world – our friend, agent, adviser, secretary and keenest supporter. He was to become the most respected man in Barrow, and his voice as familiar to me as the Redifon man-pack radio set which I tuned up every night. It was through his calm assurance and diplomacy that our many American and Canadian friends never lost faith that the Expedition would ultimately succeed, despite the many setbacks we faced during the crossing of the Arctic Ocean. But the radio equipment, like practically all the other gear we would require during the crossing, had still by the end of July to be bought or borrowed, and Freddie's task like mine was office-bound and hectic.

Prince Yuri Galitzine, a Public Relations Consultant and friend of George Greenfield, offered his advice free of charge together with his services and a Mayfair office space. Both offers were accepted and within a week the pace and purpose of our office work moved up another gear. An attractive brochure was produced outlining the aims of the Expedition – an appealing document inviting donations to a fund which had a target figure of £20,000. The response was most encouraging: within a few days, Charringtons, Sainsbury's and the British Sugar Bureau had each made donations of £1,000, and several smaller donations too numerous to mention came in from well-wishers and business concerns. The International Wool Secretariat, who had previously backed Sir Francis Chichester in his round-the-world voyage, encouraged us with a donation of £2,500 and a generous offer to supply all woollen clothing that would be required by the crossing party. The biggest single grant by far, however, was that of £6,000 from the Trustees of the Leverhulme Trust towards the scientific programme of Dr 'Fritz' Koerner, appointing him as a Research Fellow.

Fritz during this period was in Ohio trying to write up the field data he had gathered from the previous summer with the Americans in the Antarctic at the Pole of Relative Inaccessibility. His wife Anna was expecting their first child – the baby was due within days of the date set for the Expedition's departure from Barrow, and Fritz's wish to stay with Anna until after the birth was causing some concern to the Committee and close supporters of the Expedition in London. Most of the exchanges between Fritz and my office in London were, however, regarding the instruments he would require for his work. It was his intention during the journey to make measurements of pack ice thickness, snow depth and density, and the height and frequency of pressure ridges. He would require very little equipment for this aspect of his work, but for the heat balance studies which he hoped to make in the summer and winter he needed sensitive totallizing anemometers; thermistors and thermistormeters; solarimeters; psychrometers; a radiometer, several low-temperature thermometers and a petrol-driven generator. I had in the course of my experience in the polar regions handled none of these instruments, and in our anxiety to make absolutely certain that we purchased the right apparatus many hours were spent relaying information or seeking it.

Allan Gill's project during the journey was to be the filming; and the B.B.C., having had a change of heart, asked me to get Allan back from the Arctic as soon as possible in order that he could do a short crash course in cinematography at the Royal College of Art in London. During the winter on the Arctic Ocean, as we drifted, he would conduct a geophysical programme of ocean depth soundings, magnetics observations and gravity recordings. The ice drift would be precisely recorded by taking observations of the stars with a theodolite.

My responsibilities during the journey, apart from the leadership, would be principally those of radio communication and navigation, although it was becoming increasingly evident from correspondence between George Greenfield and our various literary sponsors that I would be obliged to do a great deal of writing during the summer and winter drift periods. I was to have this book written within one month of returning to London, and, in addition, articles of 30,000 words for *True* magazine, of 6,000 words for *The Sunday Times* and 3,000 words for the International Wool Secretariat. I should perhaps have considered taking a ghost writer as the fourth member of the crossing party, but it was the consensus of opinion in Committee on the 31st July that we should try to find a doctor.

I made a direct approach to Major-General John Douglas of the R.A.M.C. a few days later and was told that the R.A.M.C. were very short of doctors – indeed they had only two that might care to consider joining the Expedition, one was a gynaecologist, the other a captain in the Special Air Service. The latter was phoned up by the General and asked if he was interested – Captain Hedges replied that he would consider it and, having put the receiver down, called in his sergeant to ask him what he knew about the Arctic Ocean. His sergeant remembered having seen some reference to the Arctic Ocean in *The Sunday Times* a few weeks before, but the paper had been thrown in the trash can. Fortunately the trash had not been carted away, the newspaper was found and the article written by Peter Dunn read with interest.

Ken Hedges was a few months younger than me. Born in January 1935, he had spent his early childhood in the Fiji Islands where his father was a Government architect. He returned to England at the age of five to live near Southampton, where he attended the King Edward VI Grammar School. At the age of fifteen he entered H.M.S. *Worcester*, the Imperial Nautical Thames Training College. He served a short period at sea on the Far East run to Japan, but left the Merchant Navy and shortly afterwards was hospitalized for nine months

as the result of a serious traffic accident in which he broke a leg
and both arms. His interest in medicine dated from this period
and he began studies at Bournemouth Municipal College for
the G.C.E. 'O-Level' which he got without difficulty.
'A-Levels' followed in the autumn of 1956 and so admission to
the University of Liverpool as a medical student. Some nine
years after changing his vocation, he graduated M.B., Ch.B.,
and became house surgeon at the Royal Victoria Hospital,
Boscombe near Bournemouth. He entered the Royal Army
Medical Corps in 1963, and in the years between 1964 and 1967
was the regimental medical officer of the 22 Special Air Service
Regiment. Ken Hedges from his *curriculum vitae* was evidently
a great outdoors man, having also been a sailing instructor at a
Y.M.C.A. summer camp in Massachusetts, U.S.A., an instructor
at the Outward Bound sea school at Aberdovey, and an
instructor of the Duke of Edinburgh's Award Scheme. He was
a military parachutist, a frogman, and had seen active service. It
was, however, not possible to interview the short list of four
applicants for the post until the 19th September when, by
unanimous vote of the Expedition's Sub-Committee, Ken
Hedges was offered the place on the crossing party vacated by
Roger Tufft. Meanwhile, we who were deeply involved in the
Expedition had survived many a crisis – most of them financial.
The lowest ebb was reached on the 6th September.

No foundation could be found willing to underwrite the
Expedition and it was the general feeling of Barclays, the
Expedition's bankers, that it would be unreasonable for them
to carry all the risk at that stage in the Expedition. They felt
that if they committed themselves to lending a part of the total
sum required, they might, if the Expedition was unable to raise
the remainder from industry or private sponsors, be obliged
to put up the remainder themselves; it being, therefore, a
question of all or nothing, they were reluctant to help. A
tentative suggestion was made on the 6th September that it
might be safer to postpone the Expedition for a year whilst its

finances were put on a firmer footing. At this point an emergency meeting of the Committee was called. In effect, we had three months left in which to turn the £50,000 expected for the most part from copyright contracts into cash to meet our commitments.

Two hours before the emergency meeting with the Committee, I was called by Mr Pirie-Gordon to a consultation with his colleagues at Glyn Mills & Co. In answer to several searching questions there was a consensus of opinion given in nods by the bankers around the table. Mr Pirie-Gordon was thus able to tell the Committee that Glyn Mills were prepared to advance up to £15,000 provided Barclays matched this with at least another £15,000. The Expedition at that point in time was born.

Now, for the first time in four years, it seemed likely that the Expedition might get off the ground financially. There was, however, always the possibility that it might founder during the first few hundred miles or, as the more sceptical of our critics predicted, might not even set foot on the Arctic Ocean. Well aware of the risks involved in making a pioneer journey across 3,800 route miles of drifting ice, our various literary sponsors had taken care to safeguard themselves by making payments by instalment, the bulk of the money needless to say not being due until the Expedition had successfully completed the journey. Our bankers, by taking as their security the sum total of those literary contracts, accepted a greater risk in underwriting the Expedition; but was this risk not covered by Lloyd's, with whom the Expedition took out insurance at a premium of over £7,500? And what of those private sponsors and friends who chipped in a few hundred pounds or even a few shillings at a time when we most needed it? They had no thought of commercial gain and made their donations on no security at all. Surely it is to them we owe the greatest tribute, for it was with their money we paid the premiums on the insurance which covered the bankers. But then, would Lloyd's have taken on the risk had the Expedition not had the backing of the B.B.C., *The Sunday Times* and the indirect support of several Government departments? Or had we as members of our Committee men of lesser prestige or business acumen? The more I consider the financing of this Expedition, the more I come to regard our sponsors on near equal if not equal terms – as friends, as opposed to the detractors and critics of whom, not surprisingly, we had many.

We had opposition of a more positive nature too. We had heard rumour that an Australian, Mr David Humphreys, was in New York organizing a joint American-Canadian Expedition which, with dog teams, would set out by the shortest axis to make an attempt at the first surface crossing of the Arctic Ocean in December 1967. Fløtum, the Norwegian, as far as I knew was still intent on making a crossing of the Arctic Ocean from Spitzbergen via the Pole to Ellesmere Island. Bjørn Staib was rumoured to be planning another attempt at the Pole; so too was Ralph Plaisted, the latter once again with motorized sledges. There was also a German, whose name we never did learn, who was, so we heard, having a running battle with the Danish authorities to set off from a base in Peary Land (North Greenland) in an attempt to reach the Pole with snow-tracked vehicles. We took few of these reports seriously, for we were far too involved in our own affairs and in the ordering of equipment to waste any time in corresponding with our competitors.

In order to simplify the massive task of equipping and victualling the Expedition we concentrated our orders in batches. All foodstuffs were handled by the ships' victuallers, Andrew Lusk Limited, and both our sledging rations and our winter supply which was far more varied and bulky was based on the diet of the British Antarctic Expeditions – a diet familiar to Fritz, Allan and me. The clothing, including that supplied by the International Wool Secretariat, and general camping equipment was handled by Graham Tiso of Edinburgh, who, in addition, acted as our agent for obtaining a few items of gear which he did not stock, thus saving much time in correspondence. The dog food – a concentrate of whale meat, dried yeast, skimmed milk powder, pre-cooked maize starch, beef dripping and various vitamins – was specially prepared and packed by Bob Martins Limited, 33,000 lbs of it, at a cost of just under £5,500. Four modified Eskimo-type sledges and four wider, heavier and much stronger sledges based on the Nansen design were built by Skeemaster Limited of Great Yarmouth. Special sledge boxes were constructed, dog harnesses made up, medical gear selected and packed; cameras, film, tape recorders – the telephone was seldom in its cradle, there were crises all the time, deadlines to be met. The responsibility weighed heavily on Frankie Ryan and me for we knew that, once on the Arctic Ocean, if any item of equipment had been forgotten it would have to be improvised; and in spite of the many long lists we made we were always left with the feeling that something had been forgotten. I went back on to the tranquillizers but they made me sleepy, and so thick and fast did the crises occur I just had to regard the pills as a luxury and for the time being give them up.

I was during this period trying to write a book and an article – both were commitments which at that time seemed impossible to meet. I had by that stage developed a habit of working strictly according to my own set of priorities, the Expedition being top of the list, allowing myself to be distracted only by those who made their presence felt. Howard Cohn, the Managing Editor of *True* magazine, evidently sensing this in New York, flew to London. Every morning for a week I would meet him for a working breakfast, during which we would go through what I had written the previous evening, take leave of him for an hour or two and plunge deeply into the affairs of the Expedition. At my office, in which he made himself at home, he would spend most of the day behind a typewriter transcribing notes he had taken – notes which were an invaluable help when I was able to snatch a few minutes to work on the article. It was finished with a flurry of hand-written insertions in the passenger lounge of London Airport five minutes before he boarded his plane. *A World of Men* was completed on the deadline. Allan Gill arrived in London direct from the Canadian Arctic and started his course at the Royal College of Art. I flew off to Edmonton, Alberta, to talk with two commercial charter air companies about the Expedition's air support requirements and to meet, in Ottawa, General John Allard, Chief of Defence Staff. The latter had been most dis-concerting when I entered his office with a letter of introduction from Air Chief Marshal Sir Charles Ellworthy, Chief of Air Staff, Ministry of Defence. 'What do you want?' he asked in a friendly tone of voice. There were no minutes taken of this meeting and I cannot now recall, precisely, how I worded my request, but the result of my visit was the support of the Canadian Forces – a relationship from which I believe we were both greatly to benefit.

Which part of my letter, of 25 September 1967, to Sir Michael Cary (Permanent Under-Secretary for the Royal Navy) carried weight I cannot say. I marshalled many argu-ments why the Royal Navy should participate in the enter-prise, pointing out that Spitzbergen was a theatre of operation in which the Royal Navy had for two centuries excelled.

It was from Spitzbergen that Captain the Hon. Con-stantine Phipps in 1773 made his attempt at the North Pole, a voyage on which there was among the young gentlemen of the quarterdeck, a Midshipman Horatio Nelson. It was from Spitzbergen that Edward Parry made his attempt at the North Pole, in 1827, setting a record furthest north for the Royal Navy that stood for fifty years. Spitzbergen was the traditional British route to the Pole and it is therefore only right and proper that it should be a Royal Navy vessel that supports this Expedition on its approach to Spitzbergen.

The Royal Air Force was already represented on the Expedition by Squadron Leader Church who, in addition to manning a relay station and passing the Expedition's weather and general traffic, was to conduct a programme of research for the Royal Aircraft Establishment into very low-frequency radio propagation. Redifon and the Signals Research and Development Establishment were providing the radios. The Royal Aircraft Establishment's experimental radio station at Cove was to act as base radio station in United Kingdom. The Army were represented on the Expedition by Captain Ken Hedges, R.A.M.C., and the Royal Canadian Air Force had agreed to provide the air support for the crossing party. It was no surprise therefore, but none the less a relief, when the Royal Air Force solved the biggest of our current problems – how to get all our gear to the two Arctic staging depots.

Two flights were to be made by an R.A.F. Hercules. The first, on the 28th December, would leave from the R.A.F. base at Lyneham and fly direct to Resolute Bay; the second, on 6 January 1968, would fly with Squadron Leader Church and the remainder of the equipment to Thule, where it would collect Allan, Ken and forty dogs and continue to Barrow, Alaska. How we managed to collect all that gear, sort it, pack it, and have it transported by road to Lyneham, I cannot recall. My memory of that period is a confusion of blurred images, the ringing of telephones, and insuperable difficulties all of which were solved.

Ken and Allan left for Point Barrow on 12th December. I arranged to join them early in January. Seventy thousand pounds of food, fuel and equipment was assembled, sorted and packed in Britain and air lifted to Resolute Bay in the Canadian Arctic and to Point Barrow, Alaska, by crews of the Tactical Hercules Force of the Royal Air Force, Lyneham. The forty Greenland huskies had been purchased on behalf of the Expedition by Inspector Orla Sandborg over a period of several weeks from the many isolated Eskimo villages which are in his care and jurisdiction in the Thule District of North-West Greenland, and these were collected by Allan and Ken over the Christmas period of 1967.

In company with a few Eskimos, Allan and Ken had driven the dogs seventy miles in total darkness from Qanaq to the air force base at Thule to a rendezvous with a Royal Air Force Hercules on the 6th January. It had been, for Ken, his first sledging journey – a tough initiation for the medical officer of our party who, as a doctor with the British Army Special Air Service, had spent most of his time in the jungle and hot deserts. For Allan, that winter journey was nothing unusual; in company with Roger Tufft and myself he had spent the previous winter at Qanaq whilst Doctor Fritz Koerner, the fourth member of the crossing party, had been with the American Expedition in the Antarctic at the Pole of Inaccessibility. Furthermore, Allan, like Fritz and myself, had spent several winters with scientific stations and other expeditions in the Arctic and the Antarctic; he was an old hand at the business of handling huskies and knew by sight and name most of the regulars who spent time in the Arctic outposts. The air transportation of the dogs to Barrow via Resolute Bay had therefore gone without a hitch, and the Royal Air Force Hercules had been met at the airstrip by several of Allan's Eskimo friends. With their help the cargo had been shifted to a huge warehouse, a step or so away from the laboratory, and the dogs to an isolated spot two miles south-east in a dismal but well-heated hut which Dr Max Brewer had kindly made available to us; here we could thaw out and chop walrus meat, brought by the Eskimos, as food for our dogs. These buildings over the last few weeks had become scenes of great activity. Our massive supplies of rations, dog food, equipment and fuel had been stacked in four loads and every item checked and rechecked. Our dogs were sorted into four teams of ten, and two snow-tracked vehicles were put at our disposal in order that we could more frequently visit them and shift cargoes of carcasses and walrus meat out to our satellite station. We were also given the use of a room at the laboratory where we could work into the early hours of each morning on reports of the ice data and official correspondence. Our sledges were modified in the carpenter's shop and relashed with the help of the Eskimos.

Our dog harnesses were adjusted and restitched by their women, and our fuel decanted into jerry-cans. Our radios were checked, tents were erected, dog traces made up and star shots computed to check our navigational records. We had made frequent short sledging trips out on to the sea ice and had camped out on several occasions to shake down our equipment and wear the newness off our clothing. We had worked at fever pitch to get everything ready and were left with no time to write letters home; no time to relax, no time or patience to listen to those who warned us of dangers we had already considered; for we were too deeply committed, too determined, too wound-up to wait one day longer than necessary. It was a period which, in retrospect, I now regard as the most testing thirty days of my life.

For four years the Expedition had been in the planning; for me, four years of full-time work from the first seed of the idea to the eve of our departure. To the north, not two hundred yards away, was the Arctic Ocean, its surface as unstable and perhaps as unsafe as any comparable area on earth. Our proposed journey along the longest axis, which would take us sixteen months to complete, would be a pioneer journey, a horizontal Everest that would dig so deeply into our reserves that it would mark each one of us for life. Our beds, most nights, would be on ice no more than two metres thick; ice which might split or start to pressure at any time. There would not be a day during the next sixteen months when the floes over which we were travelling, or sleeping off our fatigue, would not be drifting with the currents or driven by the winds. There would be no end to the movement, no rest, no landfalls, no sense of achievement, no peace of mind until we reached Spitzbergen. Guided by the Committee of Management of eight eminent men, each with far-ranging interests and influence in the City, the Expedition had signed contracts with *The Sunday Times* and *The Times* of London for exclusive newspaper rights, and with *True* magazine for the magazine rights in the United States. We had signed contracts also with the publishing houses of Longmans in London and Putmans in New York for the copyright of the book, and with the British Broadcasting Corporation for the television rights of the film. The Expedition had been granted the status of a non-profit company, had been given the support of the Royal Geographical Society and the backing of bankers and industry. It had been honoured by the patronage of H.R.H. Prince Philip and the vice-patronage of the Rt. Rev. the Lord Bishop of Norwich and Sir Raymond Priestley, proclaimed by the press, adopted by the public, encouraged by scientists and promised logistic support by the Defence Ministries of Great Britain, Canada and the United States, this before the first walking step had been taken. Such a brainchild dare not falter or be heard to cry for help.

By midnight on the eve of our departure the pace of preparation had slackened. It was like the eve of a battle – still, clear, cold, silent, with no one sleeping, an atmosphere heavy with private thoughts. Fritz had spoken to his wife, Anna, on the telephone earlier in the evening and had promised to phone her again the following morning. He was in his room now sorting through his papers and carefully packing his instruments. Ken and Allan were also pottering with their gear. A mile away, in Freddie Church's radio shack, I was making my report to Sir Vivian Fuchs who, throughout the long preparations, had been one of my strongest supporters. I was speaking to him in his London office through the Expedition's United Kingdom Radio Headquarters at the Royal Aircraft Establishment Experimental Station; ten days short of ten years after the snow cats of the Commonwealth Trans-Antarctic Expedition, of which he was the leader, had rumbled into Scott Base at the end of their epic journey.

I believe he noticed the excitement in my voice, for he, perhaps better than anyone, knew with what feelings we were struggling during those last quiet hours before dawn. I had been through all this so often before during my long polar career, but somehow this was different. Alone in the warehouse, loading the sledge, I found myself obsessed with the struggles and hard times of the past few years, the crises, the depressions; and how, but for the faith of my parents, a few close friends and the encouragement of my colleagues, the dream with which I had lived could never have taken place and become a reality. The Expedition for me was already half over; for Allan and Fritz and Ken it was about to begin.

6 Start from Barrow

I UNLATCHED THE HUGE DOORS OF THE WAREHOUSE AND
SPREAD THEM OPEN – THE NIGHT WAS ALMOST OVER. IT WAS
calm, clear and very cold. The sledge moved over the floor
on rollers, bit the snow and slid forward. I left it and walked
up the street to the Mess Hall, where I met Freddie Church
and the others. We ate breakfast leisurely, smoked for a while,
then got up and left.

We drove for the last time out to the hut we called the 'dog
house' by way of warehouse No. 37, the four loaded sledges
being towed by a snow-tracked vehicle bearing a whole hoard
of cheerful people. Already we could see a sprinkling of folk
waiting at the 'dog house' to see us off – these were the hardy
ones who had walked out the three miles. The majority, we
knew, would be waiting at the rocket-launching site about a
mile to our north-east. It was a matter of only a few moments
to hitch up the dogs and take up position in line ahead for the
first short stage of the journey; hardly time enough to feel any
sensation other than that of a pounding sledge, and in no more
than ten minutes we had drawn alongside a sizable crowd
of well-wishers who had come out from the laboratory
and the Eskimo village in relays of truck loads and private
vehicles.

They were a motley collection, perhaps two hundred in all.
Most of them were in khaki parkas with enormous fur hoods.
Some had their hands in their pockets, others were gently
pumping their arms to keep themselves warm. A mist of
breath vapour hung like a low ceiling over the whole gathering

of curious spectators standing, it seemed, a respectful distance
from a funeral cortège of four identical coffins which during
their long slow journey had momentarily halted. In due
course, a few of them stepped forward to take photographs
and a few of them shook us by the hand; but even Freddie
Church and Dr Max Brewer stood strangely subdued and
mournful.

When we moved away they were still standing, silently, as
they had stood on our arrival. A few of them, almost too late,
waved farewell like puppets; then their arms fell as if the
strings had been cut, and in a moment they were lost in a pall
of vapour created by our teams of dogs. I turned away and
looked east for a while at a blurred horizon. The wind bit into
my face. I pulled the hood of the wolfskin parka across my line
of vision and huddled deeply into a protective shell of fur. By
sundown we had travelled only five miles with the lights of
Barrow still in view, but we were on sea ice and well satisfied.

From what we had seen on the ice reconnaissance flight, our
only chance of crossing the fractured zone north of Barrow lay
in a detour to a point sixty miles to the east. In that vicinity the
belt of mush ice which marked the northern edge of the landfast ice was at its narrowest, about half a mile wide. Elsewhere
the line of shearing was less distinct, for the whole area had been
worked over and had cracked open so many times that the
lines of shearing were themselves cut to pieces. There was no
certainty that the route we had chosen would hold together
but it was calm and the air temperature was minus forty
degrees Fahrenheit. The omens were good; so we set off in high
spirits to put the first sixty miles behind us before noon on the
25th February.

This first target we achieved not without some hard sledging
and, at mid-day on the 25th February we climbed the highest
pinnacle for a view of the ice to our north. The prospect was
utterly depressing: as far as the eye could see there was chaos –
no way seemed possible except the route by which we had

come. For the rest of that day and all the next we hacked road-
ways northwards and hauled the sledges over ice rubble, rafted
slabs and massive walls of pressure. On the night of the 25th,
we camped on thin ice. On the night of the 26th our two tents
were pitched one hundred yards from a ridge which formed the
south wall of a channel choked with pressure ice débris and
huge ice blocks. There was no movement, no slush, no sign of
water. Bathed in the pink glow of sunset that evening, the
mush ice belt had seemed tranquil enough; but a better route,
we felt sure, would exist further to the east.

Several times during the next two days we were forced to
retrace our steps and set off in a new direction but we made
progress and, except for the loss of one dog which had been
killed by the others, we were well pleased with events at our
camp site on the 29th February. Even the rumbling and creaking of the huge pressure ridge three hundred yards to our south,
across which we had hacked our way a few hours before, drew
no more than a casual comment as we went about the task of
pitching our camp in a cheerful frame of mind.

The sun was setting. It was dead calm. There was hardly a
cloud. Had I not been outside the tent at the time, not one of us
would have been aware that the floe had split. It looked almost
as though unseen blades had slashed the ice in a movement
quicker than the eye could catch. The splits ran parallel and on
either side of us: the strip on which we were camped was no
wider than twenty yards. We hurriedly broke camp, but in the
fading light the strip on which we were standing came off,
cracked at right angles and reduced the area in which we could
manœuvre the dogs and sledges to a pan of ice sixty feet by
eighty. There was no escape route east, west, or south; our only
chance was the pressure field to our north. We persuaded the
dogs by the whip to leap an open lead – those who hesitated
were thrown or pushed in and forced to swim a few struggling
strokes. The sledges all dipped in for a moment as the dogs
dragged them across, but none of the equipment on that

occasion got wet and we re-pitched our tents about one hundred yards from the site we had abandoned. By that time it was pitch dark.

We slept fully clothed and kept watches for the rest of the night, and, as dawn approached, I ventured from the camp. Not two hundred yards to our north was a vast area of open water. To our west, about fifty yards from our tent, was a small north-south lead which linked up with the open water to our north and south. What a precarious spot it must have looked to Bob Murphy when he flew over us that morning in one of the Arctic Research Laboratory's Cessnas. Several times he had flown over us in the past few days. Occasionally he had offered us advice on the best route out of some particularly confusing maze of pressure ridges, and had undoubtedly saved us many hours of hard and fruitless work; but on this day we needed more than a route – we needed some idea of the general nature of the ice cover to our north. We suspected – and it was so confirmed later by Bob Murphy over the radio – that the whole area was breaking up. He passed us another piece of information that to us came as a complete surprise: in the last forty-eight hours we had been carried fifteen miles to the west. As to our immediate course of action, we had little choice – we broke camp and sledged due east.

By late afternoon we reached a flat stretch of ice which had that morning been projecting like a prominent cape into the sea of open water. The far shore meanwhile had closed in, but the currents were moving in opposite directions at about three knots, and at the point of contact a spectacular ridge of pressure was building. Huge slabs of ice were creeping in jerks up the sides of a twenty-foot moving wall from the inside of which came groans and agonized, muted, screeches. Blocks of ice weighing several tons tumbling from its summit and shaken from its sides fell with roaring dull thuds and the sound of sliding shells as the ridge moved forward over the débris it was spreading before it. But the rate of movement and the direction seemed fairly constant, so we moved on two hundred yards at right angles to its line of advance and set up camp.

It was dusk before we were inside the tent, and dark outside by the time we had prepared our evening meal. In a warm fug we were relaxing. We could hear no noise of pressuring above the roar of the primus stove, nor at first could we believe Fritz's shout of alarm that the pressure ridge was only thirty yards away and bearing down on us. The tent suddenly had become a tomb and the sleeve entrance our only chance of escape. We grabbed clothing down from the apex and dressed, stuffed our gear into bags, heaved them outside and plunged out after them into the night. Dimly lit by an auroral glow, the advancing pressure looked like a crumbling wall of alabaster. Black sea was boiling at its base. You could feel dull shocks through the ice as enormous blocks slid forward and thudded on to the floe. The noise was getting louder – the profile of the ridge climbing higher – we could smell the sea. Gear was thrown on to the sledges and lashed in a desperate hurry. The dogs were hitched up, and the yelling, cursing procession moved off into the pressure hummocks of the rougher ice to our south.

I saw ahead of me three pricks of yellow light bobbing and swinging. I could hear every muted word crystal clear. Behind me I could sense the nearness of the pressure ridge and hear it chewing up the small patch of smooth ice which had been our camp site. The aurora was brighter now and washing the sky with strokes of light, writhing, convulsing and radiating spears of brilliance. The icescape had taken on a green-grey magical quality, but it faded in time and turned black.

For six hours we struggled, cursing our dogs and working the sledges over unseen obstacles in a fruitless effort to put ourselves out of earshot of the pressure. At times we seemed to be surrounded by the noises of grinding ice. Cold and exhausted, we pitched our tents and stood watches. It was dead calm, the sky was clear, the temperature was minus forty-one degrees Fahrenheit.

At the first light of dawn I took my rifle and set off to scout around. We did not seem at that time to be in any immediate danger; but Bob Murphy, circling over us in his Cessna a couple of hours later, could see that the floe on which we were camped was splitting and urged us to move in a hurry back along our tracks to a spot not three hundred yards south-west of the pressure ridge from which we had escaped the previous night. The ice to the north of the ridge was still moving west, but at a slower rate. There had also been a change in its appearance; it was jostling, fracturing, being ground into mush, and while the mist swirled around us all that night and the following day we took it in turns to rest.

On the morning of the 4th March, twelve hours after the movement had ceased, we drove our teams on to the mush ice. It now extended for three miles – a sea of débris and mush knit together by a thin film of ice. All that was needed was a five-knot wind from any direction, or for the big floes on either side to shift a few degrees and the thin film of ice would have shattered. We spent a few tense hours on that fragile surface and the sledges, men and dogs broke through several times before we reached the safety of an old floe. It was really only a fragment of a polar floe, perhaps a couple of hundred yards across, but it was the first of its kind we had seen. It had the undulating surface of an old weathered piece of ice which had apparently survived several summers and drifted many thousands of miles.

It was the 15th March before we met another, and by that time we were in need of rest. Only two days before I had written:

This morning we crossed the only big lead within thirty miles of Barrow that was still frozen. All around us the ice is opening up and for several days we have been on a treadmill of floes drifting westwards towards the open water area north of Barrow. We have had a few adventures and the occasional hard-won success, but we have generally been out of luck. Today we came closer than at any time in the past three weeks to reaching relatively safe ice, but we were stopped short by opening leads. Tonight we are as usual standing watches and are prepared to move at a moment's notice. But tonight our situation is particularly unhealthy. The floe on which we are camped has been cut off from the safer ice to our north and, with a steady drift set in motion by several days of north-east wind, we stand a good chance of being taken for a ride, a dangerous ride westwards. With one good break we could safely get on to the polar pack and start making mileage. We have about three hundred and fifty miles to pull back before the summer re-supply – I believe we can do this given a minimum of four inches of ice.

That note of optimism at the end was perhaps as characteristic of my confused feelings at that time as the message I composed to Dr Max Brewer the following day in a more depressed mood on the subject of logistics:

At our present rate of progress it may be several days before we reach safer and presumably faster going. By then we will be over four hundred miles behind our scheduled position and out of phase with the five phases of the Expedition. It seems, at its very worst, this slow progress of ours could affect seriously the entire scheme of things – it could mean that we will not reach the right latitude for our summer camp and in consequence drift in an unfavourable direction. We would be thrown even farther out of phase by not making enough northing during the autumn, and this in turn would leave us with such a great distance to cover during the spring of 1969 that we would fail to reach Spitzbergen before the sea ice breaks up. In other words, we could, by cumulative delays, be as much as a full season out

of phase and find ourselves in the late summer of 1969 drifting on a pan of ice into the Greenland sea.

The way I saw it, at the time, there were only two solutions:
we might increase our daily mileage by stumbling upon a series
of frozen north-south leads about which we had been told so
much; or we might attempt travelling throughout the months
of June and July, a period when most polar travellers would
prefer to be on dry land. The first of these two solutions would
be pure luck, but the second, logistically, could be prepared for.
In the original plan, the Arctic Research Laboratory were to
have made the first two re-supply drops, and the Royal
Canadian Air Force the next five. By some adjustment to
the dates, but without increasing the number of drops, it
would be possible to extend our travelling period, and this
change of plan, with the goodwill of our supporters, was
adopted.

By the end of March we seemed to have got clear of the last
of the dangerous coastal currents; but although we were making better progress, it was not across polar pack as we had
expected but mostly across extensive areas of fractured new ice.
There were, however, encouraging signs. Temperatures were
still in the minus thirties, old floes were becoming more
frequent, and the action of the drifting ice more predictable.
We were beginning to regard as normal situations which three
weeks before would have alarmed us. Our sledges had taken a
tremendous hammering without so much as a hair-line crack
in their solid oak sides. The dogs, too, were getting into their
stride and although two more had been killed from the original
forty there was, if anything, more power in the teams. It was a
relief, also, that the re-supply aircraft were finding us without
difficulty and that we were beginning, consistently, to better
our daily target of ten nautical miles a day. In fact, not until
the 5th April did I record any obstacle to our steady progress
towards the Pole of Relative Inaccessibility:

Our position fix last night (8th April) put us at latitude
74 degrees 49 minutes north, longitude 158 degrees 45 minutes west – that is about two hundred and fifty statute miles
from Barrow but only one mile north of our position of
three nights ago. We have been forced fifteen miles off course
to the west by an open lead and are now in a region where
the polar pack is very active. We cannot afford these delays
if we are to be in the vicinity of the Pole of Relative
Inaccessibility by Midsummer's Day. The target ought to be
easy enough – in a straight line it is eight hundred and ten
statute miles from Barrow, and the pack ice on a direct
course should be drifting about half a mile a day in our
favour; but so far we have detected no such drift or it is lost
in the crudeness of our dead-reckoning system. We drive our
dogs on a heading of three hundred and thirty degrees, true,
but often detour as much as twenty degrees to avoid
obstacles. We steer by the sun. We compute our position
from precise altitude observations of the sun. There is nothing
else visible in the sky except the moon – the stars have all
gone and it will be many months before we see them again.
Can't help wondering where we will be then.

We had sledged about nine hundred route miles by the time
we received our first, thirty-day, re-supply from the Royal
Canadian Air Force on the 10th May. We had seen how the
ice behaved in the spring, and had been on young icefloes when
they had split. We had sledged across vast areas of ice barely
thick enough to support the weight of a sledge – areas which
only a few days before had been seas of open water. We had
struggled from winter into early summer across mountain
ranges, lakes and islands, rolling hills and dazzling plains – an
icescape at times chaotic and yet sometimes so tranquil, so
deceptively still, it was hard to believe that the mountains were
no more than thirty feet high and the sea beneath our feet ten
thousand feet deep. But our sledges were showing signs of

wear and my three companions, limping along behind them, looked weatherworn and tired. Metal plates held together long splits in the runners, and splints and lashings were holding together the broken handlebars. We reached latitude 80° N hopeful that we would never again encounter travelling conditions as terrible as those we had met in the last sixteen days. The weather and the ice had deteriorated, the snow was deep and sticky, the skies were overcast. We had hacked our way forward, often in 'whiteouts' over fractured ice and pressure fields worse than anything we had seen in the mush-ice belt off the Alaskan coast. We had come upon open leads every few miles and averaged only two miles a day. We had been forced to convert our sledges into boats in order to ferry dogs and gear across leads which could not be crossed on ice rafts or bridged with pressure débris; but at 80° N we met an impasse which deflected our course north-east into the influence of unfavourable current.

We were carried eighty miles off course to the east as we struggled in a hopeless maze of shattered floes to maintain a north-west heading. Cracks and leads we were now meeting every few hundred yards. The whole vast area was in motion, slowly swirling, eddying – a confusion of currents, counter-currents and winds which moved the sea ice like brittle scum in a stagnant pool stirred from below. We progressed across the chart through six degrees of longitude, fighting for every mile and travelling at night to avoid the daytime temperatures which occasionally went above freezing:

It is Midsummer's Day – the day, a year from now, when we hope to reach Spitzbergen having successfully achieved the first surface crossing of the Arctic Ocean; but we are a long way behind schedule. Four months ago today we left Point Barrow; four men with four teams of dogs and a journey ahead, the outcome of which few even of our friends would favourably predict. Less sympathetic but more shrewd were those who remained non-committal, for the conditions we met and our rate of progress has at times been very frustrating. At noon today our latitude fix showed 81 degrees 18 minutes north, an advance of only half a mile on our position of two days ago. This puts us at the same distance from the Pole of Relative Inaccessibility as Shackleton was from the South Pole in 1908 at the time he and his companions turned back. I doubt if we will get much further this season for the old floes now are badly split; black sea-pools and leads are spreading like a stain – we are travelling on borrowed time.

Our last seven days before setting up summer camp on 4th July at latitude 81° 33′ N, longitude 165° 29′ W, were physically the hardest of the whole journey. We drove the dogs out of their depth in wet snow and melt-water pools, and had to drag them out one by one. We put two teams together and drove them through on extended traces with all four of us pushing, stumbling and shouting ourselves hoarse. The icefloes were by that time a shimmering maze of melt-water pools and leads. In places there were cracks every fifteen yards. Each day the pools were deeper and the dogs more reluctant to plough their way through, dragging a sledge. We were fighting a losing struggle with the drift – a hopeless effort to travel north-west in search of a safer area in which to sit out the summer melt. We had come a long way. Since leaving Barrow on the 21st February we had sledged one thousand one hundred and eighty route miles.

We had sledged further from land over the polar pack ice than any other travellers. We had measured floe thicknesses and snow densities almost every day. We had kept logs of wild life, and logs on the type and ages of the ice across which we had travelled. We had recorded synoptic weather data which we had coded and then transmitted daily to the fifth member of the Expedition, Squadron Leader Freddie Church at Barrow;

he, in turn, had passed it on to the United States Weather Bureau and the British Meteorological Office. Sadly, we had failed to travel far enough for we were still in the influence of a current circulating to our east; but we had reached our limit and could do no more.

7 Summer Camp

OUR TENUOUS LINK WITH THE OUTSIDE WORLD WAS A THREE-FOOT CABLE CONNECTING A HAND GENERATOR TO a nickel cadmium battery, the power supply for a remarkable transceiver, the Redifon GR345. With this portable high-frequency radio, which has a peak power of only fifteen watts, we had, since leaving Barrow, been transmitting daily progress reports and weather data. This information was received and passed on by the fifth member of the Expedition, Squadron Leader Freddie Church, who acted as our liaison with the Royal Canadian Air Force and the U.S. Naval Arctic Research Laboratory on whom we depended for support.

Using a Collins KWM2A transmitter and amplifier, with a peak power of about a kilowatt, these progress reports were also relayed by him to the Royal Aircraft Establishment's Experimental Station at Cove near Farnborough; here these signals were received by directional antennae and recorded on magnetic tapes. Within a few minutes the messages would be passed to Sir Vivian Fuchs, the co-ordinator of the Expedition's activities in London, and through his office to the other members of the Committee.

A small number of amateur shortwave stations in the United Kingdom, acting as a 'back-up' to the Radio Station at Cove, handled the Expedition's weekend traffic, and our link to Barrow was backed up in poor radio propagation conditions by other enthusiastic amateur radio operators on the American drifting station T-3, and the Canadian Arctic Weather Stations in the Queen Elizabeth Islands.

Only at the source was the system vulnerable. It was here, in the three-foot cable which connected the hand-powered generator to the radio batteries, that we discovered a wire had broken.

The consequences of a complete radio breakdown had, of course, been seriously considered as long ago as April 1964 when the plan for the crossing had first taken shape. But if in London this was a sobering thought, much more sobering was the isolation we felt when faced with the possibility of radio failure on a drifting icefloe eight hundred miles from Point Barrow. Our radio beacons, which attracted aircraft like audible magnets, had a limited battery life and we could, in the event of a radio breakdown, only afford to switch them on between set times for a quarter of an hour each day, starting from the fifth day after the last radio contact. Bearing in mind that the party was drifting, and that the drift was unpredictable, even knowing what speed and in which direction the wind was blowing; and considering also the error of an astrofix made from the support aircraft, the problem of estimating a time of arrival at a point eight hundred miles away, without knowledge of the wind along the flight path, was great, and the chances of finding the party was, at the very best, evens. We would need to drift only about ten miles to be out of the aircraft's target area; and to be found by systematic search, the aircraft would have to cover an area of some 1,600 square miles.

Amongst the tracery of shadows, cracks and open leads, four men, two small tents and thirty-six dogs would be almost impossible to see. There had been occasions during this journey when aircraft had flown within half a mile of our camp without seeing us. Other occasions when aircraft had been even closer before we had heard their engines. What then were our chances of survival?

The Arctic explorer Vilhjalmur Steffanson had a theory that

Picking route across lead

Melt season: waterlogged ice

The first sign of life, a gull, since leaving land

Old polar ice denuded of snow

Pressure ridge: tilted block of ice

Closing lead near summer camp creates pressure ridge

Ken rescuing dog from lead

The summer camp, 1968. Parachute tent in foreground

Left: Fritz measuring wind and temperature profiles. *Below:* Allan operating hand generator. Remains of polar bear in foreground

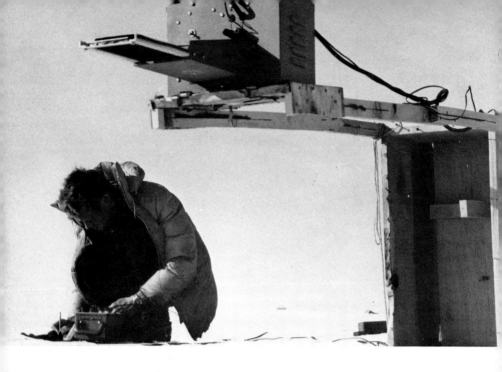

Fritz measuring solar radiation

Winter quarters by moonlight

Wally in winter quarters, operating radio

The dogs, feeding time

Wally Herbert

man could survive by hunting in the Arctic Ocean. We had yet to put this theory to the test, for each airdrop, up to then, had arrived on time with food and fuel in excess. We had seen both polar bear and fox tracks during the journey, but the animals themselves kept out of our way, and the total of twelve seals we had sighted in the previous five months, together with four gulls, a little auk, two long-tailed jaegers, and a flight of ducks, would hardly have made a respectable feed for our thirty-six working dogs.

We were discussing this at the time when the break in the generator cable was found – it was fixed with a home-made soldering-iron and the subject of survival dropped.

Our position at that time was latitude 82°27′ N, longitude 163°30′ W. 'Meltville,' as the press called it, the world's most remote and insecure village, had been set up on the 4th July. No further travel was contemplated on the 3,800-mile crossing from Barrow to Spitzbergen until the autumn freeze-up, but the floes were not only melting – they were jostling and fracturing. With more open water space, the floes were moving faster, but although our perch was somewhat precarious it was neverthe-less a consolation to be drifting due north at a rate of about five miles a day.

'Meltville' was a village of two pyramid tents and a marquee which we had made out of five parachutes from the fifty-odd that had settled on our floe a week before from the massive summer re-supply drop of the R.C.A.F. We had built our-selves furniture, chairs and a table, out of packing-cases and empty boxes. It was rough, crude carpentry. We had to pinch nails from boxes and hammer them straight, but the result, although not attractive, was functional.

For the first time since leaving Barrow, we delighted in sitting at a table and eating a variety of food. The cooking was fairly basic. It was either fried or boiled, for we had no oven at that time in which to bake bread or roast the many chickens dropped to us by the Americans from the Arctic Research laboratory. They did, however, drop us plenty of bread; about four hundred loaves were used as packing for Fritz's scientific instruments. Collecting water was easy in the summer – you just went out with a bucket and dipped it into a pool. Later in the summer, you could take fresh water from the sea leads, provided there had not been any local movement in the icefloes within a period of some twenty-four hours to stir up the sea water and mix it with a layer of fresh water which in some places went down to a depth of six feet.

July 29th was one of those rare days on the Arctic Ocean when the warmth of the sun penetrates to the skin, a perfect day with temperatures two degrees above freezing: clear blue sky, not a breath of wind; the sort of day when working dogs with no work to do lay sprawled out like folded dog-skin rugs whilst their masters wasted time wondering how best they could employ them.

Our dogs had fed well the night before on a polar bear that had come unexpectedly into camp. We, still sleepy at noon from working hard into the early hours, skinning, gutting, and chopping it up, felt disinclined to do the many repair jobs needed to our equipment. There was time enough over the next three weeks to check the waterproofing of our boxes, fix the sledges, make new dog traces and generally prepare ourselves for the autumn struggle across open pack ice to the north-west in search of a favourable drift stream and an old floe on which to winter. So we declared a day of rest. This in effect relieved only three of us from our chores. Dr Koerner had a glaciological and micromet programme which kept him almost fully occupied for seventeen hours a day. He was the first up every morning and the last to turn in every night, continuously on the move across the floe from one delicate instrument to another, measuring temperature profiles through the four metres of ice below us, and the minute changes in the wind and temperature of the sun-warmed surface.

I set out with a rucksack, camera, harpoon and rifle in search of seals along an open lead while Ken, Allan and Fritz did some photography below the surface of the same lead, nearer camp. Ken, wearing a Neoprene wet suit, dived to a depth of ten feet. Fritz, who had made a very precise level of the surface, using a theodolite, was interested in the sub-surface forms of the floes, and this was excuse enough for Ken to dive with a Nikonos underwater camera in an attempt to get some pictures.

I saw no seals, but it didn't really matter on that occasion. We had fed well enough on polar bear, and the beef steaks and eggs dropped to us by the Arctic Research Laboratory a few days before. That flight, made in a Dakota by Dick Dickerson, was a remarkable piece of navigation. Dick was the pilot of the U.S. naval Antarctic flight from South Africa to New Zealand in 1963, and must have flown close to his safety margin many times in his career. But I doubt if even he had ever flown to a target so small and so isolated as our camp. It was very foggy on that day and Dick, homing in on our radio beacon and an orange smoke flare, told us he could make only one pass because of the shortage of fuel. In fact he was obliged to make five in order to despatch all the cargo. We saw the aircraft for only a few seconds on each run. Freddie Church, who was in the plane, saw nothing of us except a faint split-second outline of the tents. The 1,700-mile trip was celebrated by Dr Max Brewer and his staff back at the A.R.L. that evening, while we, eight hundred miles out on the Arctic Ocean, were enjoying an enormous feast and listening to Bach on a tiny casette tape-recorder sent out to us from London.

With that drop we also received a new radio set, and, for a while, considered ourselves safe. But at 1 a.m. that night the floe split wide open a hundred yards from our camp. The lead was still opening at 3 a.m., and grey patches on the base of an overcast sky indicated vast areas of open water all around the horizon.

Many of our difficulties rested on the deceptively frail-looking shoulders of Squadron Leader Freddie Church whose capacity for going without sleep astonished most of the younger scientists working at the Arctic Research laboratory, Point Barrow. In one of Don Banas's dispatches from Barrow to *The Times* he said, 'Freddie works as though he could never go to bed in daylight – which is permanent at present in the Arctic – co-ordinating air drops, rounding up additional supplies in the Eskimo village at Barrow, maintaining a regular radio schedule with London, coping with the awesome amount of correspondence that Herbert passes out from "Meltville" even when radio conditions are terrible. Church regards the frailties of man-made radio sets and the curse of heaven-sent radio interference with equal suspicion, as though both are a deliberate affront to his optimism and his qualities as a Service officer. He will sit, night after night, in his radio shack, jamming his hands over his earphones like a man with migraine, listening for Herbert's voice in the raucous explosion of noise caused by geomagnetic and ionospheric storms. If all else fails Church will try again, switching from voice contact to Morse, prodding through the ear-shattering crackle to pick up signals so weak that he sometimes suspects them to be more imagined than real. Invariably when conditions are bad, he instructs Herbert to reply just "R" for Roger or "N" for Negative, straining to separate his code signals from the splashes of static filling his headset. Wherever "Meltville" drifts during the next two months and whatever its four inhabitants do during the final year of their trek, Freddie Church will look after them.'

The summer for me on the whole was a very relaxed period, in spite of the fact that I had to produce 12,000 words for *True* magazine and turn a hand generator for a total of fifty-seven hours in order to provide enough power to transmit the article to Freddie. Ken used this period to measure and weigh several items of clothing as part of his clothing research programme. Allan's chief project was the navigation – once, or sometimes

twice, a day he would take a sunshot which confirmed a steady
and very encouraging drift almost due north. But our parachute
tent, where all four of us met for evening meals around the old
crate which served as a table, had become, after eight weeks, a
limp and grimy hovel; the ceiling was by then sagging around
its props. From a web of strings hung socks and gloves. There
was an odour of wet wood and stagnant water. Some of the
floorboards were submerged; others, pedestalled on slippery ice,
were wedged with tins and metal spikes. Two primus stoves
roared beneath the table. Sledge ration boxes served as seats.
We dressed for dinner in woollen sweaters and windproof
trousers, down jackets, gloves and Wellington boots. We drank
Bass with our meals and used table napkins. Our conversation
was lively but not up to date.

Our two doctors generally did most of the talking until
it was time for Dr Koerner's nap. There would then be the
usual ten-minute break, during which Ken would slip away,
while Allan, overcome by drowsiness which depressed his
shoulders, released the cigarette from between his fingers, and
dozed off without closing his eyes. Allan used to call it 'bloater's
lurg' – it would hang, so he told us, suspended and unseen
above him and would descend when the plates were stacked.

He had picked up a few wrinkles over the years in more
senses of the word than he cared to admit, and had for certain
items of clothing an intimate attachment. He was wiry and
tough and, at thirty-seven, was the oldest and horniest hand of
the party. A master of the temporary repair and the ingenious
contraption, he had, over the last ten years, spent more time in
the polar regions than any other Englishman. He had wintered
three times in the Antarctic, once in North-West Greenland,
once in the Canadian Arctic, once in Alaska, and three times
on the Arctic Ocean at the American Scientific Drifting
Station 'T-3', where he is remembered as 'that helluva-guy'
who did the bottom photography.

It had taken him three winters to perfect his technique of

photographing, in colour, the ocean bed and the turtle-like tracks of some identified creatures at a depth of twelve thousand feet. The triggering mechanism of the camera shutter and Strobe light, which sank into the ooze at the end of a thousand-pound cable, presented the sort of problems which Allan found intriguing and to which he usually found a solution.

Much of his work on 'T-3' was a routine geophysical programme conducted by Lamont Geological Observatory; but in addition to gravity measurements and magnetics, he had been involved in several other pioneer projects for Lamont which had their teething troubles, and to which he could apply his infinite patience and his self-taught knowledge of mathematics and physics. He had made seismic measurements of waves transmitted through the ice, and experimented with a lethal piece of apparatus for measuring the sub-bottom strata of the ocean bed. He had taken core samples of the mud and dredged the abyssal plain with a bucket for ooze and microscopic shells. He didn't know, nor was he too concerned about, what happened to his samples when they were sent South. He is at home in the Arctic and in his element pottering far from the pundits who would give him the answers in chalky formulae, or a more expensive piece of equipment; and I suspect he would live in the Arctic for the rest of his life if he didn't feel, as most men do, the occasional need for adventure. He then makes an expedition into the human jungle and drinks for a while at the fountain of Bacchus.

He would nod, and give an involuntary grunt, as Dr Koerner opened one eye like the blind of a bungalow window. The sun had found a hole in the clouds and lit the floe for a moment. Our large shapeless shelter cast long shadows over the surface which no longer seemed familiar, for the first snow of winter had settled on the squalor and puddles that pockmarked the surface around our camp and had transformed an icescape, wet-green and rotten, into a dazzling wilderness. Each pit and crack was now a trap, and each forest of razor-sharp crystals was now a hidden menace. We had slipped from summer into autumn. In five weeks we would lose the sun and sink quickly into winter. It was time we were moving on.

We had to find a good floe for our winter quarters before the 20th September. The floe on which we had spent the summer would not do; it was too far east to pick up the trans-polar drift stream which would carry us towards the Pole. My aim was to be at latitude 85°30' N, longitude 175°00' E, in time for the winter supply drop. We would regard ourselves lucky if we made it across such a treacherous surface.

8 Allan's Accident

THE POOLS THAT BURNED THROUGH THE FLOES WERE
BOTTOMLESS HOLES CAPPED WITH A THIN FILM OF ICE
under a soft blanket of snow; long ice-crystals like racks of
razorsharp spears carpeting the beds of drained melt-water
lakes were hidden beneath a thin covering of snow; old cracks
and leads were dangerously undercut, and intricate snow-
covered channels of slush were still knee deep in the pressure
fields and brash.

We had set off on the 4th September with heavy loads and
travelled only a couple of miles before we were obliged to
pitch camp, and in overcast weather had made even slower
progress the following day probing every foot of the way. On
the 6th, we had pushed forward four hundred yards only to
meet a mush-ice belt blocking our route north-west, and Allan
had hurt his back when trying to manhandle his heavy sledge.
We had made no progress on the 7th – the mush ice was in
constant motion and the wind from the wrong direction. But
on the 8th, determined in spite of the weather to get clear of
that dangerous area, we had moved another four hundred
yards before being brought to a sudden halt. Allan had
stumbled awkwardly and collapsed by the side of his sledge. It
was a good few minutes before Fritz and I realized that Allan
had been hurt, for we were some distance ahead trying to find
a way through the rubble of ice blocks and compressed sludge
that barred our way. By the time we returned he had 'seized up'
and was feeling very cold. There could be no question of

moving him to a safer spot. We had to put the tent up within a few yards of the sledge and bodily manhandle him through the sleeve entrance on to his sleeping-bag. He was by then in great pain.

Ken had moved into the tent with Allan, given him a morphine injection and made him comfortable. He came over a little later to tell me that he suspected Allan had slipped a disc, although he did not rule out the possible alternative of a severe muscle sprain. Clearly we had to move Allan as soon as possible to a safer spot, for the floe on which we were camped was not much more than a hundred yards across, and the tents were no more than thirty yards from the edge of the active belt of mush ice. It was decided, therefore, that Fritz and I would set off the following morning in an attempt to find the string of floes on which we had spent the summer. There was no hope of retracing our outward tracks, for our route had been smashed up behind us.

We set off into head-wind and drifting snow the following morning with two sledges, a radio and provisions for ten days. In due course we found the summer floe and, retracing our tracks with difficulty, marked the route with flags. That night I sent out a radio message to Freddie Church for onward transmission to London:

NR399. 100831Z. Herbert to Fuchs – Urgent and Confidential.

Distressed to report Gill has badly injured his back. Hedges suspects either acute slipped disc or severe muscle strain both of which are liable to recur. No question now of attempting crossing of the mush-ice belt or any further travel this season. Must return to summer floe. Found it after search today. Gill will be drugged and manhauled to summer floe as soon as possible. If no miraculous recovery within next few days will have to ask ARL to fly him out in the Cessna that brings the geophysical equipment.

On the 10th, Fritz and I made a second journey back to the summer floe, taking on that occasion a small load of expendable stores which we left in a depot about a mile to the south of the old summer camp-site. Near by we found a frozen sea pool between two floes. The ice cover was about eight inches – it was fresh-water ice, and our guess was that within a week it would be thick enough to serve if necessary as a landing-strip for a Cessna, perhaps even for a twin-engined Otter. Allan's pain was more widespread but less intense by the 11th, and he was willing to risk an uncomfortable ride in order to get clear of the active ice on which we were camped. So, after a cargo trip, Fritz and I helped Ken take the tent down over Allan's head and lift him in his sleeping-bag on to an upturned inflated rubber boat which had been lashed to Ken's sledge. Well bolstered, and protected from the elements by a rubber ground-sheet, he was driven the two miles to the old summer floe without too much discomfort.

We had of course by this time discussed amongst ourselves several different courses of action, and Ken had explained to all three of us the significance of the various tests he had done on Allan, and the possible consequences of a relapse. It was Ken's opinion that Allan should be evacuated if at all possible. Allan, on the other hand, was prepared to take the risk, and both Fritz and I, feeling that had we been in Allan's position we would have reacted in the same way, supported his view.

The big questions I, as Leader, had to face, were whether or not it would be possible to evacuate Allan during the winter, should he suffer a relapse; and whether I would be prepared to accept the risk to Allan, to the party as a whole, and to the pilots of a rescue mission, of keeping him on the ice. I naturally gave the whole problem a great deal of thought, and took into consideration many aspects of the situation. The benefits of having Allan with us during the winter, provided he did not suffer a relapse, were unquestionable: he could direct, even if he could not partake in, his programme of geophysical research; he could share with us, even if only in a sedentary capacity, a winter which we had long planned and looked forward to; and he could, provided he survived the winter, probably stay on at the hut with a Lamont Geological Observatory crew who would come out about the 1st March to take over the station and continue the geophysical work.

In answer to a request from the Committee, Ken prepared a detailed report which I transmitted on the 12th September. This medical report was passed on to the Commandant of the Royal Army Medical College. Ken sent a second medical report on the 13th. I received one on the same date from Sir Vivian Fuchs saying that the 'Royal Army Medical College state emphatically that Gill must be evacuated when possible and should not, repeat, not continue sledging even if recovered as he will remain a danger to the rest of the party'.

Fritz and I made a thorough reconnaissance of the area on the 14th and 15th, and I reported by radio to Freddie that we had found a good site for the winter camp about half a mile from a lead in any direction. The floe we had found was about a mile and a half square. It was, however, surrounded by a number of broken-up floes, and a small amount of pressure was building up. On the sea pools around the floe I reported that we had found a number of long level strips, the best two of which were about half and three-quarters of a mile long respectively, but they both needed to thicken up considerably before they could be used. On the 17th September I informed the Committee of my decision to let Gill

. . . stay with the expedition right through to March 1969 when he will be relieved by the geophysicists from Lamont Geological Observatory. In view of the great distances that must be travelled next spring and Gill's incapacity, I am absolutely convinced that the dash to Spitzbergen must be made by Koerner and myself. As a two-man party we would travel harder, faster and more efficiently than as a three-man unit. Hedges will therefore remain with Gill at winter quarters until relieved by Lamont geophysicists thus enabling Koerner and myself to set out earlier. In this way the journey and the scientific programme of the expedition can be completed and all four men will fully have contributed to the Expedition's ultimate success.

Evacuation in the event of a relapse would not have been difficult, since the expedition was only one hundred and fifty miles from T-3 which could be used as a staging-post. The winter is the normal flying season for air operations on the Arctic Ocean, and an airstrip could easily be lit with candle beacons and marker flares. On 20th September I received a message from London:

Committee discussed all known factors including communications and beacons. While recognising Allan's great wish to winter we regretfully decided that on medical grounds and to enable earliest possible start next spring, he must, repeat, must be evacuated in Phipp's plane. A three-man party is regarded as the minimum acceptable risk, therefore Wally, Ken and Fritz to winter and complete journey. We appreciate this may mean abandoning geophysical programme if spring landing to recover instruments cannot be made before journey resumed. Lamont should be warned of this problem. Letters written yesterday to be delivered by plane will indicate the thinking which prompted Committee's decision.

In reply, I acknowledged that the Committee was in a better position to review the Expedition's financial situation, and to set limits on the scientific programme if it seemed too costly. I asked with the utmost respect that in future, in response to requests for moral support or any change of plan which concerned the physical act of crossing 3,800 miles of drifting pack ice, or in answer to any notes informing the Committee of any intended course of action on the same subject, that the Committee, in deference to my responsibilities and in respect of my experience and judgement, send me recommendations not directives.

On the 25th and 26th September we received our massive winter supply drop from 435 Squadron R.C.A.F. The drop was an outstanding success. Out of the three C130 Hercules loads, totalling twenty-eight tons of cargo, the only loss was a dozen bottles of HP Sauce! We had come to rely on the R.C.A.F. not only for our supply drops but also for the moral support and encouragement we needed in order to survive. We sensed this encouragement in the care taken to check our equipment, the many thoughtful gifts and the shouts of the dispatchers standing in the open cargo door as the aircraft made its final low passes over the camp.

I sent a message to Freddie Church that night:

. . . We are now sorting out twenty-eight tons of stores and equipment – boxes all around us. Main landing strip I spoke of a few nights ago now cracked up and unusable. There is another fresh-water ice lead eight to nine inches thick, one hundred and fifty yards long and thirty yards wide, but this has new pressure ridges on each side of it up to fifteen feet high. Landing strip on floe covered by six inches of snow and will take some time to clear. Understand Weldy Phipps proposes to use his twin-engined Otter with small wheels – recommend strongly he fits skis. We have a mass of gear to shift and now strongly suggest you delay Weldy's flight to us until 30th September or the 1st October. Please tell Peter Dunn to inform Richard Taylor of the B.B.C. that I seriously believe the ice could break up at any moment and that there is a very real risk that Weldy may not be able to get back to pick up any reporters or B.B.C. crew that are landed at our position.

It had long been the intention of *The Sunday Times* and the B.B.C. jointly to charter Weldy Phipps, a Canadian Bush Pilot, to fly out from Resolute Bay in his twin-engined Otter and land at our winter camp-site. The B.B.C. crew were to take film of the erecting of our hut and our preparations for the winter sojourn on the ice – *The Sunday Times* reporters were to interview us. Perhaps, had they come out, many of the embarrassing reports appearing in the national press round about the 25th to 27th September might have been answered and put right in one short accurate account of our situation.

ROW OVER ARCTIC EXPLORER [read the banner headline in the *Daily Mail* for 25th September]. . . . A row broke out last night over the four-man British Trans-Arctic Expedition, which is now about three hundred and thirty miles from the North Pole. The organizers in London issued the statement saying that the leader may be suffering from 'Winteritis'. This is a condition 'which clouds the judgement and can become a danger', but the leader, Mr Wally Herbert, whose dog-sledges are now two-thirds of the 3,800 miles between Alaska and the Norwegian Island of Spitzbergen, hit back with fierce criticism of the Organising Committee. In an interview with *The Sunday Times*, Mr Herbert said over a radio link: 'The Committee are getting completely carried away with themselves, sending directives when they should be sending recommendations'.

MY SON WOULD WANT TO STAY ON THE ICE-CAP, SAYS FATHER – the banner headline in the *Yorkshire Evening Post*. 'We think Mr Herbert is not himself – *Daily Mail*, London, 26th September.

You are crouched in a tiny tent on an ice floe three hundred and thirty miles from the North Pole. Outside a hurricane rages at 120 m.p.h. Outside you cannot see a yard in front of you in the blinding snow. Outside your dogs in the sledge team bite and snarl at each other. Inside you huddle for warmth against your three companions. One is injured. You are off course, and behind schedule. The eyes of the world are upon you. This is the agony at this moment of Wally Herbert, leader of the British Trans-Arctic Expedition, the loneliest man in the world in the earth's white graveyard. What effect can such appalling conditions have on the mind and morale of a man? Do they explain the terse messages Herbert has been sending back to the Expedition's Organisers in London?

These were the opening words in an article entitled 'In the Arctic Blizzards, Even a Man's Mind Can Freeze Up' by Donald Gomery of the *Daily Sketch* for 26 September 1968. Or yet another: 'If You Ever Just Sit and Stare Blankly at the Office Wall . . . then you could have "Winteritis". Wally Herbert, leader of the British Trans-Arctic Expedition, may be suffering from "Winteritis" says the expedition's London Organisers. They describe the condition as one which "clouds the judgement and can become a danger" ' – Peter Pringle, *Evening News*, 25th September.

With so much drama and so much speculation, it is hardly any wonder that the interpretations of our behaviour were at times a little bizarre. Peter Dunn, *The Sunday Times* reporter who was to have flown out to us in Weldy Phipps' twin-engined Otter, and was at that time geographically closer to us than anyone else, made his own personal assessment of our situation in a dispatch to *The Sunday Times* on the 6th October:

Breaking ice, bad weather and snow driven across the Arctic ice cap by a gale-force wind, foiled an attempt this week to evacuate Allan Gill, the 38-year-old injured Arctic walker from his camp eight hundred miles out on the polar pack ice. Gill, who severely injured his back in a fall a month ago, will now spend the long dark winter with the other three members of the British Trans-Arctic Expedition and will be lifted off next spring before the final stage of the 3,800-mile trek from Alaska to Spitzbergen. The attempt to evacuate Gill which was ordered by the Expedition's Committee in London, was called off after a three-day wait with a twin-engined Otter aircraft on T-3, an American research station perched on the coast of a vast slab of drifting glacier ice. This station is only one hundred and fifty miles from the Expedition's winter camp-site.

Wally Herbert, the leader of the party, could scarcely contain his delight that the landing had failed and that Gill would be staying with the Expedition till the spring. 'Morale now is absolutely terrific,' Herbert told me over his radio. 'Naturally Allan's situation is a bit worrying; he is not quite as fit as he used to be. He's got what I call a most uncharacteristic military bearing – he bends down like a woman, to keep his back straight. We'll mark out an emergency landing strip in the next few days before it gets dark and keep it in pretty good trim during the winter. Then, if Allan has a relapse, we'll be able to get him out OK.'

Gill's accident caused a thunderous row between Herbert and his London Committee. When the Committee overruled Herbert's plan to evacuate Gill next spring, Herbert shot off a broadside about people who 'didn't know what the bloody hell they were talking about'. The Committee responded by saying that Herbert appeared to be suffering from 'Winteritis', an Arctic condition 'which clouds the judgement and can become a danger'. Their diagnosis seemed a trifle abrupt to some observers here in Barrow. Herbert has his faults – a Napoleonic sense of drama, impetuosity and a tendency to think too much in a loud clear voice – but he is a long way from going barmy. He wanted Gill to stay for the winter because the Arctic is Gill's life and any alternative, death included, would be preferable to the stigma of failure during an expedition.

Twenty-four hours after receiving the Committee's order to evacuate Gill, Herbert noticed that the landing strip was breaking up around his camp. Even the thicker ice-floe landing area was becoming unapproachable due to heavy snow falls – 'a hell of a job to clear' Herbert said. Out on T-3 we heard Wally report difficulty with his hand-operated battery charger which charges his radio batteries. Then his voice faded away and further contact was impossible. Next morning, a fairly clear day for observations from the aircraft, we had an early radio date with Herbert in which he was to have reported on a further reconnaissance around him. Unfortunately, although we could hear Barrow radio eight hundred miles away on the Arctic coast, we didn't hear Herbert who was on the same frequency one hundred and fifty miles to the west of us. Herbert's radio improved amazingly when the landing became unthinkable. He was at that point in excellent form.

Herbert now has everything his own way. Gill stays out until he wants him to leave. The scientific equipment which we took to T-3 for the Expedition's winter programme has been lugged back to Barrow and will be parachuted to the Expedition's winter camp by the Arctic Research Laboratory. A particularly delicate instrument has been left on T-3 and will probably be landed at the camp by one of the laboratories' highly skilled bush pilots. The general opinion here seems to be that the fuss over Allan Gill got a little out of hand: whatever happens this winter, Herbert will not be short of friends on the North Alaskan coast and he will not need aircraft support directed from London.

Had I been able to get through on that occasion by radio, I could have told Peter one day earlier that the ice had broken up. As it was, I was obliged to send over the radio a much longer message on the 8th October 1968, in an attempt to get the whole furore in perspective:

A590. 090740Z – Chairman from Herbert – My message of the 17th September offering the Committee a plan by which both the scientific programme and the journey could be completed was based on the hope that it would be possible for the geophysical apparatus to be delivered by ARL Cessnas and that Gill would be permitted to stay with the expedition through the winter.

This message was marked PERSONAL AND CONFIDENTIAL. In it I recommended that Hedges remain with Gill at winter quarters in order that, first, the scientific programme could be completed and the hut handed over to the Lamont relief and, second, that it would be possible for Koerner and myself to start early on the long trek to Spitzbergen:

I remain strongly of the opinion that this proposal is feasible and far more desirable than the alternative of abandoning the geophysical programme, and evacuating Gill before the start of the winter.

I must stress that this plan would be unnecessary if an aircraft could make a landing at winter quarters at the end of February to collect the data, film and scientific apparatus which needs recalibrating, and to bring in the Lamont geophysicists. I must stress also that such a landing may be possible. In this case Hedges would join Koerner and myself in the final dash to Spitzbergen; and Gill, if he is given the Committee's permission to winter over, would remain with the Lamont crew at winter quarters to continue the geophysical programme. I can assure the Committee I have no intention (and never have had) of taking a high-handed and arrogant stand regarding these recommendations.

At great lengths by letter I will endeavour to put my proposals and will accept the Committee's advice on all matters on which they have to hand sufficient information.

If this advice is contrary to my opinions I will put my case more fully by cipher and lengthy messages.

There is no disturbed thinking on my part nor is there any lack of respect for the Committee in spite of the remarks made by me in spontaneous frustration on the 22nd September and quoted verbatim in *The Times* and other national newspapers strictly against my wishes. Without the Committee this expedition could not have been launched or conducted so successfully to date – without clear judgement on my part and the extreme physical effort of the crossing party it could not have reached this latitude. An alternative explanation for my 'behaviour over the last few days' must therefore be found. For like my remarks of the 22nd September, the reference to 'Winteritis' was no doubt also spontaneous.

For half an hour every day for the last eight months I have spoken on the radio to Squadron Leader Church, the fifth member of the Expedition. Rarely have I been aware during these conversations of the distance which separates us for I have grown as accustomed to his radio voice as I have to the mannerisms of my three travelling companions. We pass our traffic and comments on the day's events as between friends in the relative privacy of a frequency seldom used at that time of day, and in the knowledge that there are very few eavesdroppers with receivers sensitive enough to monitor my transmissions. Nevertheless we guard our remarks and on occasions use cipher to protect the interests of the Expedition, its Committee and its sponsors. On only one occasion, in frustration, have I made spontaneous and angry criticisms, and that indiscretion was provoked by the message from the Expedition's Committee on the 22nd September directing me on medical grounds to evacuate Allan Gill.

Gill is one of the easiest men to get along with that I have ever met, and temperamentally is the ideal companion for a long and arduous sledging journey or for a winter drift in a hut isolated six hundred miles from the nearest land. He is calm and confident in a crisis. He works hard and seeks no glory. He regards the Expedition as an extension of a way of life he has led for over ten years, and measures the consequences of a relapse of his injury (from which he is making an uneventful recovery) against the demoralizing alternative of being sent out, perhaps unnecessarily.

He is prepared to occupy himself throughout the winter in the sedentary aspects of our scientific programme, and to resist every physical activity which might aggravate his condition. But even thus restricted I know he will be happier here than anywhere else, and his contribution to the expedition both from the point of view of his morale and its scientific programme would be considerable.

I was, and still am, prepared, should the Committee permit me, to take the responsibility for his evacuation if during the winter he suffers a relapse and evacuation becomes necessary.

Gill and I know each other well. We trust each other implicitly. He is the most loyal friend I have. Is it not therefore natural that I should support a man who is prepared to take the risk and with whom I have shared risks and hard times in the past? We did not undertake this journey unaware of the risks, and we must take many more if we are ultimately to succeed.

But these reasons excuse only my spontaneous and frustrated comments at the time of receiving the directive from the Committee. The indiscretion of making them over the radio is inexcusable, and for this I apologize.

Had my remarks been less spontaneous they would have reflected more truly my relationship with the Committee with whom I have worked in harmony for two and a half years and for whom I have the highest regard. Had they been less spontaneous they would have been less quotable, and far less often quoted.

9 Winter Camp

THE FLOE ON WHICH WE HAD SPENT THE SUMMER HAD
CHANGED CONSIDERABLY IN THE SEVEN DAYS WE HAD
been away. Blizzards had packed the snow down and even the
débris of the summer camp was almost buried. In our search
for a suitable place for our winter quarters we had several big
floes to choose from; we were also looking for a flat stretch
on a floe which we could use as an airstrip. By the 15th
September we were satisfied we had found both.

There had been a beautiful sunset on that day and Allan,
whom we had transported successfully from the scene of his
accident to the old summer floe on a sledge covered with an
inflatable dinghy, was well enough by then to contort himself
for a look out of the sleeve entrance of the tent at that rare
phenomenon in high latitudes. By the time of the R.C.A.F.
airdrop on 25th/26th September he was up and about.

The airdrop itself was a most impressive spectacle. The two
C.130 Hercules, having made their first low pass of our camp
in formation, had separated and taken up stations a few minutes
apart and systematically peppered our chosen floe with seventy
parachute loads of supplies. Richard Taylor of the B.B.C. and
his filming crew were on board one of the C.130s, and I had
taken the opportunity of warning him that the ice conditions
were not good for the twin-engined Otter landing. They were,
however, most anxious to try and would be setting out from
Resolute the following day on the first stage of their long
flight to T-3.

Gathering together all the essential tools and sections of the winter hut took much less time than we had expected. With three of us working hard at the store hauling, Allan occupied himself usefully on repairing the damaged floor-sections of the hut. In less than eight hours' work on the 28th, we had laid the floor.

The floe we had selected for our winter quarters was about a mile and a half in diameter and surrounded by other floes of smaller size. The whole nest of floes covered an area of about five square miles, each floe separated from its neighbours by a strip of mush ice. The hut in its crates had been about 5 feet by 13 feet long and had been dropped in one enormous load with three parachutes. Separated into individual crates, it had been sledged to the site. This had been a fresh-water lake during the summer which had now frozen over, and on this perfectly flat surface we laid the foundations for the floor.

The construction of the hut was very simple: the packing boxes themselves we used as a floor, and their contents were constructed around them. This was basically a frame, covered with padded blankets, which had two windows at each end and one door leading to a small porch. The hut went up very quickly, once the floor was laid – about nine hours as I recall. The floor dimensions were 15 feet by 15 feet, but since the hut was cylindrical in shape the effective area was somewhat smaller than a small room in a house. It was of course at that time bare of furniture, and we guessed rightly that it would be just a little cramped for four men by the time it was cluttered with furniture and gear. On the other hand, we did not want too much space otherwise it would be too difficult to heat.

The heating arrangement was a Coleman space heater, a kerosene-burning stove which had an exhaust pipe running upwards for about 5 feet before turning through a right angle out of the hut. With the stove roughly in the centre of the hut, and the exhaust pipe travelling some 15 feet of hut space, we had the benefit of an extra source of heating – in fact, this pipe at times became very hot. During the whole winter there were never any more than three occasions when we used any other setting on the fuel-flow control but the lowest possible one, and at times the temperature at the top of the hut would be as high as 80° or 90° Fahrenheit. On the floor it would be below freezing, but at the sitting position it was a comfortable living temperature of about 60° Fahrenheit.

We had no covering on the floor. We had thought of using coconut matting, but snow from outside brought in on our boots would in due course have been trampled into the matting and in time have packed into ice. The advantage of a clear floor was that it could be mopped up occasionally, and the ice got rid of easily. On the 8th October I was able to transmit a message to the Expedition's patron, H.R.H. The Duke of Edinburgh, informing him that we had established winter quarters on the 6th October at latitude 85°00′ N, longitude 162°00′ W – 950 statute miles from Barrow, Alaska, and 550 miles from the nearest land. My message continued:

During the next five months, whilst we are fully and usefully occupied with our scientific programme, our hut, which is situated on an icefloe at present one mile in diameter and three metres thick, will be drifting and, if our predictions prove correct, will by 1st March 1969 be at latitude 87°00′ N, longitude 150°00′ W. From that position, providing the crossing party sets out three weeks before sunrise and resists the temptation of trying precisely to locate the North Pole (in the vicinity of which we expect to be on or about the vernal equinox), it should be possible to reach Spitzbergen or a rendezvous with H.M.S. *Endurance* before Midsummer's Day.

A corner of the hut had been allocated to each man who, according to his needs and temperament, had furnished it with wood salvaged from the packing crates which, a few days earlier, had been rained down upon us.

Major Ken Hedges, the medical officer of the Expedition, had characteristically been the first to get himself organized. With one deft movement he had upturned the packing crate alongside his bunk. This box, with only one side missing, served for a few days as a writing-desk and, with a few shelves hammered inside, as a storebox for clothes and personal gear. Set up over the foot of his bunk he had constructed shelves, the back board of which served as a partition between the kitchen alcove and this piece of furniture. It was itself a sort of an alcove and looked not unlike a small altar.

Fritz Koerner's furniture, unsymmetrical and cramped, looked very cosy but somewhat rickety, whilst my own, covering three square feet of floor space which was more than my fair share, was a robust-looking piece of carpentry incorporating a writing-desk and a set of shelves built around four radios, two tape-recorders, cameras, books and navigational tables. On the floor space, immediately in front of my bed, I had laid out a sheepskin on top of a horsehair mattress. Charts of the Arctic Ocean mounted on plywood boards were strapped to the sloping ceiling of the hut; rifles hung near the door. Drying woollens, anoraks, wolverine mitts, wolfskin parkas and pressure lamps hung from the hut's ribs. It was a hut aromatic with the smell of newly baked bread and noisy with the clatter of carpentry; a hut in which there were only three beds, for Allan slept outside.

At the time of establishing winter quarters, Allan's sleeping habits made good sense for it was at that time still warm – the temperature was about minus 10° Fahrenheit. It became for Allan a habit, and by the end of the winter he had slept inside the hut only one single night, our last night at winter quarters. So his corner, instead of having a bunk there and furniture, was just bare. Nevertheless, Allan regarded this as his territory and not unnaturally didn't want anyone else's stuff in his area. If it was to be a shambles, he naturally preferred it to be a shambles of his own equipment. Generally we didn't go in for personal things like photographs. There were no pin-ups and not a single picture until towards the end of the winter when Fritz put up a coloured picture from one of *The Sunday Times* magazines, a Matisse I think. The only other things of a decorative nature that were put up in the hut were some Christmas cards which Ken had been sent in the summer-time in anticipation of Christmas; he had saved them up and brought them out and stuck them on the door on the festive occasion. We had no other Christmas decorations.

The actual building of the hut had been done so quickly that we were sleeping in the hut about three days after the air-drop, and were thoroughly squared away by the end of the first week of the winter. In a random scatter around the floe we had laid five depots of food and fuel, sledges, tents and camping gear. The dogs were tethered down-wind of a quadrant of virgin snow reserved for Fritz's micrometeorological instruments, air sampling apparatus and thermocouple wires.

During all this activity Allan was playing quite an active part. He was very careful of course that he didn't lift boxes when one was watching, but there had been plenty of jobs he could manage – furniture-making, pottering in the hut sorting out gear, doing navigational fixes. He was eagerly looking forward to starting his geophysical programme which would involve three hourly gravity and magnetics readings, and ocean depth soundings. Ken had already started his comparative study of wool and synthetic fibres. During the summer he had measured the volume of the various kinds of footgear; he now took accurate measurements and weights of all the various items of clothing that we would wear during the winter, and organized a clothing diary in which each item worn by each member of the party would be recorded by the individual together with his subjective comments. Meanwhile, all three of them had taken enthusiastically to a thunderously energetic series of exercises to keep them physically fit. It was probably all this running on the spot that, on the eve of the 20th October, had triggered the fracture that had split our floe down the middle!

The fracture had cut through the camp thirty feet from the nearest team of dogs, separating us from two of our five depots of food and fuel, and reducing what was the largest floe in the area to a segment just under half a mile wide. By the afternoon of the 21st October this segment had shattered at the north and south ends, and hairline cracks running parallel to the main fracture had further reduced the area of the floe to a strip half a mile by 250 yards. A mile to our south-west there was a fractured area that for several weeks had been in a constant state of movement. To our west and north-west, two major fractures separated us from the partly healed remnants of the floe on which we had spent the summer; the third fracture separated us from the floes to our south-east and east. In the north-east, however, the prospect seemed more promising. Once beyond the shattered area, Fritz and I had found ourselves on a sizeable floe across which we had driven our teams of dogs for about twenty minutes in darkness without meeting any pressure ridges or fractures; and it was to that floe the following day that we set about moving our hut, complete with all its furniture and clutter and twenty-five tons of food, fuel and equipment.

The track over which we sledged to and fro in darkness for ten days became a polished highway, and the sight of our winter quarters was soon a desolate spot marked only by a few mounds of wind-packed snow. The fracture from which we had escaped was soon frozen over and snow drifts covered all the smaller cracks. Within a few weeks there were no signs that the floe had split or that four men and thirty-five dogs had for a short time inhabited that spot.

By the 4th November, with the moon full and high, we could for the first time since the sun had set see the floes around us. They looked very peaceful in the pale glow of moonlight but our hut, like an ear pressed to the ice, missed not a sound and the muffled booms and pistol shots had never seemed more ominous or our camp more vulnerable.

We probably lost about a month's work by the evacuation of our first winter quarters site, for although the move itself took only a few days, re-establishing a routine was not an easy matter.

We simplified our general chores as much as we were able. For example, we had no need to wash our clothes; we had stocked our winter quarters with so much clothing that we could afford to chuck away anything that needed washing and replace it with something new. We had a sponge down in the summer time and an occasional sponge down in the winter, but we didn't make too much of a habit of washing. We never indulged in the luxury of baths for the simple reason that water was scarce. Surprisingly enough, we were never aware of any unpleasant smells; and as for the toilet arrangements, there were no restrictions other than the immediate vicinity of the hut and the quadrant of virgin snow in Fritz's scientific compound. One had the freedom of choice of site anywhere within two miles of the camp. We used to try to keep things reasonably tidy, of course. For instance, all the 'gash', tins and boxes that were to be chucked away, were put in a box and given to Fritz to dispose of when he went on his tours around the floe with his dog team. This he did every day throughout the winter, for part of his scientific programme was to keep under close observation the activity of the neighbouring floes. The boxes he used as markers around the perimeter of our floe. But there were two other good reasons why they should be taken away from the hut: anything that is left lying around creates a drift and just speeds up the process of burying the hut; the second reason for shifting the boxes was that in the summer, when the ice melts, all the stuff would then have come to light and been a source of embarrassment to us had the Lamont

Geological Observatory sent out a crew to take over our hut and continue our scientific programme.

I would estimate that a quarter of our winter was spent in surviving; collecting snow, cooking, washing up and so on – these chores we took it in turns to do, each man's turn coming round every fourth day. If one worked conscientiously at these chores and cooked an elaborate meal, there was scarcely any time left during the day. Baking bread, pastries, and three meals a day, and generally acting as mother to three hungry men, was a very tiring job. This duty to the community could not be escaped but was in time more efficiently handled. As we realized that winter was slipping away, our workload increased and we began to prepare for the final stage of our journey.

Fritz's programme was pretty well the same programme he had conducted during the summer, except that it was extended in both the number of observations and the parameters; but of course, during the winter his radiation levels, wind and temperature profiles, sea temperatures and sea salinities were all different from those he had recorded during the summer. His additional programmes included snow-pit statigraphy, ice crystallography, aurora observations and air sampling from a site upwind of the camp, samples which in due course would be studied for contamination by particles of terrestial origin and traces of cosmic dust.

The generators and battery bank were Allan's department. With the Tiny Tiger two-stroke generator, kindly supplied by the Arctic Research Laboratory as a standby, we ran the Honda generator for approximately six hours per day to operate the air-sampling apparatus, recharged the radio batteries, the electronic flash and movie lights, and a great assortment of scientific instruments. Allan's geophysical programme unfortunately never got fully under way. The magnetometer which he found to be malfunctioning he repaired, and the oscillograph for recording the ocean depths he had recalibrated and set up in readiness, but the programme of soundings could not commence because, unfortunately, for logistic reasons, the explosives could not be sent out to us. He did, however, succeed in taking six hundred observations of magnetics during the course of the winter drift, and this in itself, even if not related to the ocean depth and the gravity, makes a very interesting record. So do the observations for position which Allan took throughout the winter almost every day.

Ken's clothing programme, which I have already mentioned, needed a tremendous amount of time if it was to be done properly. We would have been obliged, for instance, to sit outside for a total of twenty afternoons, or spending each of those afternoons sitting in an unheated tent with one less layer of clothing than we needed for comfort. You had to get cold, but not quite cold enough to shiver; you had to get to the stage when you were just beginning to feel numb, and Ken would then take readings from the many devices which were secreted about the body in order to measure the heat flow and the humidity level in various parts of the clothing.

Ken's programme of psychological tests involved answering several standard questionnaires, probably totalling about six thousand questions; these questionnaires we filled up at several stages during the journey. It would take about six or seven hours to complete a questionnaire and the accompanying I.Q. test. There was inevitably a slight temptation to be facetious in the answers, and I think we all found it a little disconcerting that, in trying to answer the same questions on different occasions, we found it almost impossible to remember how we had answered on the previous occasion, and felt irritated that the psychologists would find our different answers fascinating.

A breeze from the south-west was recorded in Fritz's meteorological log at 1900 hrs G.M.T. on the 1st November. At the time he made the entry I did not recall him offering any comments, or any comments on the subject by Allan who had at that time (9 a.m. local on the 1st November) crawled out of his sleeping-bag, shaken the hoar frost out of his hair, dressed, and staggered across from the cold tent in which he had been sleeping out, to our warm hut for breakfast. Nor did it occur to me later in the day, while I was driving my dog teams back along the tracks to the site of our first winter quarters, one and a half miles to the south-west, that the cutting breeze in my face was not the breeze of movement but an unfavourable wind. Our position was then latitude 85°48′ N, longitude 164°20′ W, our farthest north in a drift that for four months had been consistent almost to the point of being monotonous as it steadily closed on the Pole at a rate of two and a half miles a day.

Sooner or later it had to turn; but not until the 9th November did we regard as unusual the shift of wind which was carrying us eastwards. On that day, Fritz, Allan and I had set off with two teams of dogs to check the state of the ice to our north, whilst Ken, whose turn it was to do the cooking, stayed at base. We had expected to find the neighbouring floes smashed up or badly fractured, and we had taken with us two hurricane lamps on each sledge, and enough equipment and supplies to keep us going for a few days.

As an extra precaution we had added to what otherwise was a light load, a radio, a theodolite and a set of navigational tables, but the precaution on that occasion had proved unnecessary, for to our surprise all the floes were tight and all the cracks healed. Even the belt of loose mush ice we had been trying to cross at the time Allan injured his back was by the 9th November well knit together and offered no obstruction. We crossed it in moonlight and continued on a northly heading until we were some ten miles from our winter quarters. We then turned for home, convinced by what we had seen that the wind driving those floes was no freak, but a far more significant change. We resigned ourselves then to the probability of being blown a lot farther to the east before the winter was through.

Our position on the 27th November was latitude 85°02′ N,

Wally Herbert

Allan Gill

Setting out from winter quarters

Towards the North Pole

The North Pole: Wally, Fritz, Allan, Ken

Homeward bound

Polar bears approaching camp

A polar bear interrupts the journey

The kill

Ken's dog inspects the bear

Open ice conditions nearing land

Major sledge repairs

Little Blackboard Island

Wally greets Capt. Buchanan of H.M.S. *Endurance*

Right: Loading sledge
on helicopter of
H.M.S. *Endurance*.
Below: Aboard H.M.S.
Endurance: Wally, Fritz,
Ken, Allan

longitude 149° 30′ W. We had been carried exactly one hundred miles to the south-east in the past twenty-six days, and the wind was still blowing. The American Scientific Drifting Station T-3 was now only 103 miles to our east-south-east. We were slowly closing in on it all the time, in spite of evidence from the 'shadowing' effect of our track and their's that both stations were caught in the same general weather system.

Even had the wind changed direction the following day, and blown us due north which was unlikely, we would not have drifted beyond our farthest north latitude of the 1st November until Midwinter's Day. It was tempting but pointless to guess where we might have been had our favourable drift continued. Nor was it healthy to brood on how the adverse drift of the last three weeks might have affected our chances of reaching Spitzbergen before the ice broke up. There were still three months of the winter to go – time enough for the wind to change and for many other problems to introduce themselves. In the most general terms I predicted at that time that if on 1 March 1969 we were still south of latitude 87° we would be a little late in making our landfall; and that if we were south of latitude 85°, or delayed in setting out, or if we were slowed down by bad ice conditions, or caught by adverse drifts, our approach to Spitzbergen would not only be late but hazardous in the extreme. 'Who thought up this Expedition for you boys?' wrote one American mother in her letter which came down on the 13th November when the N.A.R.L. Dakota made a perfect drop in the dark – as smooth a re-supply of equipment, steaks and uncracked eggs as any we had received. She had read recently something about the Expedition in the papers, and claimed to have noticed a resemblance between us and the male members of her family. 'If employment is what you babies want, have purchased formula book for all types of employment. That you boys could be independent – existing on an icefloe with practically no existence around you except the floe rat – is not the type of life

God intended for you boys. United States best location for you boys – we need you in this country help uplift our people that they may live the same as yourselves. Teach them what has been explained to you all about your health. Why has not the Government sent an airplane to pick up you babies and the dogs and return you to this country before they kill you?' She ended her letter 'Respectfully', hoping we would soon return home from 'a plot or a conspiracy for a sinister purpose. . . . Forget the three thousand eight hundred mile walk,' she advised. 'We love and need you at home in North America.' As if in answer to her supplications the wind that evening changed direction, and we were blown due south towards Alaska.

The Christmas period was a sort of time mark, a highlight only in so far as we had a slightly more elaborate dinner on that day. Our activities otherwise were very much the same. We had plenty of gin, rum and whisky, all dropped to us during the beginning of the winter, and a fair amount of beer; but we seldom drank, our diet was varied, and the tin oven in which we baked bread was blamed for many a failure during the course of the winter. As for the hut, it was at the same time both a cosy shelter and a trap. On the 3rd February at mid-day the temperature was minus 47° Fahrenheit. Vapour from the chimney was rising vertically and feeding a thin canopy of mist which hung above the hut, partly buried by the drifts of snow. To the south there was a faint hint in the sky of the returning sun, a bleached horizon, a pale sepia stain on the crest of a grey bank of cloud. To the south-east, and low in the sky, Venus was like a jewel. To the north, the moon was full and cold, and directly beneath it a brilliant burst of silver light spread out across the floes. The whole icescape was awash with light: cold, weird, winter light, which had transformed the pressure ice into foaming white breakers, and icefloes into tranquil lagoons. But overnight the weather changed; the sky clouded over, a strong wind got up and at 4 a.m. the floe split in two.

By the next day we had been carried eight miles south and our winter quarters, which the day before had seemed safe in spite of being 150 yards from the nearest fracture, was now dangerously situated in a wedge shape of two fractures which might at any time have pressured and cracked the ice in between like the brittle shell of an egg. On the 5th February the moon set. We would not see it again until the 21st February – the date, a year before, when we had set out from Point Barrow, Alaska, and driven four teams of dogs on to the Arctic Ocean at the start of a sixteen-month journey. We had then been in high spirits, confident that if we survived the first hundred miles of the treacherous young ice off the coast, we would, by the first melt season, have pulled back the distance lost by setting out three weeks late. We had been stopped well short of the first target by deep slush and vast areas of open water. We had been stopped short again in the autumn when Allan injured his back. It had happened only two days after we had abandoned our summer camp in an attempt to correct our course, and put ourselves in a better position for the start of the winter drift, and had as a consequence during the winter been carried by an unfavourable drift 120 miles off our course to the east.

By the 5th February we were 350 miles behind schedule and no nearer to our destination than we were from our original point of departure. The journey ahead seemed formidable. To reach the north shore of Spitzbergen, we would have to travel as far in a hundred days as the distance we had to date covered in just two weeks short of a year. And to get there ahead of the melt season, we would have to abandon our winter quarters two or three weeks before sunrise and force march the entire 1,300 to 1,500 route miles. To set out this early would entail travelling at the coldest time of the year, in temperatures maybe as low as minus 60° Fahrenheit.

To set out this early would also mean travelling with maximum loads, for the Arctic Angel Squadron of the R.C.A.F. was not scheduled to make the first of the three re-supply drops during the final stage of the journey until the 25th March. We would, by setting out that early, be obliged to carry with us all the way to Spitzbergen eighty pounds of exposed film, several scientific instruments and the massive accumulation of micromet, glaciological and geophysical data collected during the eight months' drift. Furthermore, not even the most experienced bush pilots were prepared to fly out to our winter quarters to attempt to land before the sun had risen. We began to feel there must be some obstruction along the imaginary line which describes a circle around the Pole at a radius of 260 miles – a hump, perhaps, over which ice drifting north could not pass. No less than four times since the end of October we had drifted towards 86° N, coming at one time to within an hour's walk of that imaginary obstacle – only to slip back again to latitude 85°30′ N, the latitude at which we had moved our hut after the first winter floe had broken up. We had hoped to establish our winter quarters at latitude 88° N, and be carried by the trans-polar drift stream across the Pole. Had this plan materialized, it would have left us with less than 600 miles to sledge to make landfall on Spitzbergen. But we had failed to get farther north than latitude 85° before we had had to turn back and return to our summer floe. And the winter drift, which we had expected to transport us to latitude 87° N, longitude 140° W by 1 March 1969, had instead carried us 130 miles off course to the east.

Nansen had faced a similar problem during his epic drift in the *Fram*. After the first eighteen months, it had become evident that the thirteen-man crew of the *Fram* were unlikely to come closer to the Pole than 300 miles unless they left the warmth and safety of the ship and set out on foot. This Nansen had done on 14 March 1895 with one companion, twenty-eight dogs, three sledges, and one hundred days' supply of food for the two men. Leaving their companions aboard the *Fram* to the more comfortable but monotonous prospect of completing the drift, and breaking free of the polar pack off the Arctic

island of Spitzbergen, they had set out due north shortly after
the return of the summer.

The frustration which Nansen had evidently experienced
during the winter of 1894-5, we had ourselves experienced
during the previous five months as our winter hut drifted east
instead of north. We, after his example, had occupied ourselves
during the drift with a scientific programme. Now, in ten days
or so, we proposed to set out, eager and a little tense.

But the polar night was rolled back too quickly for eyes
grown accustomed to the continual darkness, and the sky to the
south seemed brilliant at mid-day. On the 23rd February we felt
we could not afford to be caught by the sun. We must abandon
the station and in desperate haste escape it by sledging north
into the shadow of the earth. But that was impossible. The sun
was climbing faster than men and dogs could run, and we knew
it would start melting the thin film of ice which covers the
Arctic Ocean long before we caught sight of our destination.
We had at that time a hundred days in which to travel 1,500
miles. What possible hope was there of covering such a distance?

There was a hard-packed route winding five miles towards
the retreating gloom on the northern horizon – a blazed trail
riding the crests and troughs of the hummocked icefloes like the
wake of an ocean liner, and sweeping gracefully across the
frozen sea lakes to the chaos of ice beyond. We were almost
ready to leave that camp, to break free from the protective shell
which had suddenly become a prison. Every instinct by then
was straining for freedom, and every fibre was tense, every dog
harnessed and every sledge loaded.

10 Dash to the Pole

IT WAS ABOUT 6.30 A.M. ON THE MORNING OF THE 24TH
FEBRUARY WHEN WE WERE HAVING BREAKFAST. WE WERE ALL
packed up and ready to go but we still had several odds and
ends to sort out and the hut was in a mess. Just as we started
breakfast we heard a salvo of shots, twangy sounds which we
knew from previous experience were caused by a floe splitting
up. We dropped everything and made a dash for the door. All
four of us tumbled outside to find the floe splitting and cracking
up all around us. One crack, the nearest one to the hut, was
about twelve feet away. We weren't really dressed for outside
work and the temperature was minus 40° with a slight breeze
blowing, but we were separated from our dogs and sledges
and much of our gear. So we scattered. I leaped across the
crack and tried to get the dogs back on to our side. There
was only time for Fritz to get one team of dogs across. The
crack was opening so quickly that we all had to leap back
on to the hut side before it eventually opened up to about 45
feet wide.

Meanwhile, the whole area started to gyrate. Pressure was
building in some places, leads opening wider in others. We
weren't in any immediate danger, because once a crack has
occurred the pressure usually relaxes a little, and nothing else
happens until the floes get off line from each other and come
together again. Then you get pressure building up and cracks
occurring at right angles. This is what we really feared after
the initial crack. It had gone straight underneath one of the

two tents which had collapsed into the lead and was now lying in the water. From then on, everything was chaotic.

We rushed back into the hut. Obviously we had to get away as quickly as we possibly could, but there were several last-minute things that had to be done, such as packing up the radio set and sorting out one or two pots and pans. We didn't have time, nor did we dare, to carry on with breakfast. All the time we were inside the hut we were in danger, so we took it in turns to stay outside on guard. We threw everything into boxes and just chucked them outside. We had intended leaving the hut spick and span, sorting out all the expensive items of equipment we were going to leave behind and putting them all on the table so that if an aircraft could land at some later date, they'd be able to take the equipment away. As it turned out, everyone was in such a rush that this stuff was thrown all over the place to make room. I even had to take a hand-axe to the furniture which had taken so many days to construct, and smash it all up in order to get at the various other items of gear which were tucked away out of sight and easy reach.

It was still fairly dark outside so that every time someone left the hut, they had to take one of our two lamps, which plunged the hut into semi-darkness. All the time we were in the hut we could hear the noises of the pressure outside, and the tension grew. We eventually threw everything into four piles and started sorting it out roughly into sledge loads. The sledges had already been partly loaded a couple of days before; we had sorted out the amount of dog food and man rations we had to take, and loaded all the personal gear. The problem now was to try to get the dogs across to our part of the floe. Each man went after his own team of dogs. He had to leap from one floe to another, hitch them all up, and get them back again. The route we had taken across to the dogs was impossible to retrace because the floes were moving all the time. Some of the floes were small enough to tilt and rock when we jumped on them. One of the standard techniques for getting across leads is on a very small floe, a very small pan of ice, which can be used as a raft to ferry stuff across. You can put a sledge on to a raft of ice and get a rope on either end, with one man standing on the raft and the other towing him across with the rope.

In this way we managed to get the dogs across.

Just before breakfast that morning we had put up a flag. It was a superb, brand new, seven-foot flag which was catching the breeze and blowing out straight. Vapour coming from the chimney poured past it. It was a stirring sight, my last sight of that hut – a sinking ship in an ugly scene of gaping cracks and smoking water. One crack appeared to go straight towards the hut – it could not possibly survive, it was bound to be crushed by pressure or swallowed by another lead. Abandoning that hut was for me deeply moving. By the time we had travelled a quarter of a mile my home for two winters had disappeared into the gloom.

There was still hardly any twilight. The moon wasn't there. We had only Venus as a navigational guide, but the five miles we covered on the first day of our escape north was along a polished track.

Allan by now was in pretty good shape. He was probably fitter than any of us, apart from his back. He had been doing between forty and forty-five jump press-ups a day and had worked at his exercises until the sweat poured off him, usually outside in the cold so that he could keep his body temperature down. He, Ken and Fritz would run on the spot until I felt quite tired. For myself, I hardly ever do exercises. I find exercise as a sport unbearable. I much prefer to set off and suffer during the first few weeks of the journey than to suffer for several months in preparation for it.

Over the summer period we had caught up with the American drifting station T-3, then overtaken it, and by the end of the winter it was about 120 miles to our south-east. To take Allan there would be a waste of time from our point of view. In any case, if we could take him safely to T-3 across 120 miles of very rough ice at the worst time of year, we might just as well go 120 miles due north from where he could be evacuated – if, as planned, the Cessnas from Barrow could get out via T-3 to collect him and our scientific records and film. We could not expect them to fly out before sunrise, however; flying across the Arctic Ocean in a single-engined aircraft was too hazardous. It was very likely therefore that we would be north of latitude 88° before they could reach us.

At the time of abandoning our winter quarters we were 322 statute miles from the Pole. We soon found ourselves on very active ice and had to make several detours to get round new cracks and leads. On the second day we found ourselves in amongst pressure fields – there were only about four hours of twilight and we made little progress. The temperature was minus 40° Fahrenheit.

The first real crisis occurred on the third day out when we noticed that Allan's sledge had split along the whole length of the runner.That night we stopped to camp and make repairs. These took a long time as the temperature was about minus 45° Fahrenheit. We had to rig up a shelter as a windbreak, and use two lamps since it was too dark to see. The following day Fritz's sledge cracked, then my sledge cracked, and within a period of a week all four sledges had major splits along the full length of the runners.

The splitting was due not to bad seasoning of the wood but to the very rough going and the low temperatures which made the wood brittle. The sledges we had used from Barrow were pretty beaten up by the time we'd pitched the summer camp. We weren't at all sure that they would survive the rest of the journey. We had had four new sledges on standby, which were dropped out to us at the beginning of the winter drift, along with the hut. They were of a slightly different design, with much broader runners than the previous season's sledges, nearly three inches wide. We carried out temporary repairs on these sledges by boring holes right through the runners, fixing metal plates and inserting bolts, and lashing them up with rawhide which pulled the edges of the cracks together. All four sledges were treated thus, and to our surprise they lasted for the rest of the journey without falling apart.

It was an area with a fantastic amount of pressure ice movement. A lead would open and come together again to form a pressure ridge; then the floe would split in the opposite direction, and come together again and build another pressure ridge at right angles to it. By the time this had been going on all the winter, there would be an absolute chaos of ice. The biggest blocks were about thirteen feet high, a jumble of ice like a great field of rubble.

These were the problems in the first few days. We were only averaging about two miles a day, and at that rate wouldn't have stood a chance of getting anywhere. After one week of this I was worried. In due course, however, travelling conditions improved and we started to pick up a few more miles each day. We were still navigating on Venus, which was the only heavenly body we could see. Neither the sun nor the moon was up, but by the 9th March the clouds were catching the sunlight. The temperature then was about the lowest on the journey, about minus 55° Fahrenheit. We were travelling about eight hours a day which meant that we actually spent about ten hours of each day outside in a temperature of minus 50°, and the fatigue was crippling.

I remember some of those days very well. Looking back at the other three sledges, I would see only the plume of vapour in which they were enveloped. When we changed direction, I would catch a profile view of the three sledges, and I would see just a long stream of vapour trailing behind the panting, hauling dogs. When the sledges stopped it would dissipate, but when they were really steamed up and going, it was a tremendous sight, just like a steam-engine leaving a great plume of white mist behind it. If you were weaving through the jumbled ice or across cracks, then it would leave a weaving trail. In dead calm it would stay there for quite a long time, anything up to a quarter of an hour or more without shifting. If the sledges were coming straight towards you and there was a cross-wind, you would see a sharp-cut image of the man and his team of dogs on the one side, while on the other side there would be a great stream of white vapour pouring off them and being blown away. I remember, too, when the sun did come back and was very low. The refraction would split it into several segments, just like an orange that had been sliced. In the low rays, the vapour from the dogs would be a beautiful pink colour.

So hard was the work that, at the end of each day, we were ravenous. We needed, I would guess, about 6,000 to 6,500 calories. We were on a well-balanced diet of 5,200, but it was insufficient; and so our hunger grew, and towards the end of each day our core temperature dropped. At the beginning of the day, we were wearing quite light-weight clothing. A woollen vest and a woollen shirt and a light-weight woollen pullover and wolfskin parka. Occasionally you could work with bare hands at a temperature of minus 50° Fahrenheit; but towards the end of the day, after you'd been outside, exposed, working hard for about ten hours, you really would freeze up. The worst chore of all was making the 'ice-hole': two holes in the ice which linked up underneath like a tunnel, through which you put a rope to which a whole team of dogs would be tethered. This was the hardest part of each day because by this time your hands were so cold you couldn't properly grip the knife. Your gloves would freeze up during the day and it was impossible to straighten them out; and your mitts would assume the shape of a boxing-glove, where you had been holding on to the handlebar of the sledge. You would have to half-clench your fist before putting it into the glove. At the end of the day when the gloves – heavy woollen mitts with a chamois leather outer mitt – were removed, they'd be frozen together with condensation and you literally couldn't separate them. You'd have to thaw them out first. You'd get a knife and scrape off all the hoar frost, and hang them up to thaw out and dry.

A major problem was lack of fuel. We were trying to keep the weight down to a minimum in order that we could go for about four and a half weeks before the first airdrop. Travelling, unacclimatized, unfit, and with dogs unaccustomed to the exercise after a winter's inactivity, was heavy going and we had a very hard time for those first three weeks. They were, I think, the hardest three weeks of the journey.

There were only a few very minor cases of frostbite. Quite often we thought we were getting frostbitten because, through numbness, we would lose all sensation in our hands. When banging them together, one wouldn't feel anything. When your hands become numb the best thing you can do is to put on a pair of dry mitts; but by that time all sensation in your hands is lost anyway, and you forget about it. Under stress, or if you are on an inadequate diet, you are more vulnerable to frostbite. We were lucky to get away so lightly.

During this period, Ken had a lot of difficulty in sleeping. He used to wake up about five times each night, and when he did wake up he'd light the primus stove and make himself a brew and then go back to sleep again. It didn't affect Fritz, Allan or myself as much. I was just too tired to wake up at that time. But during the day we could usually keep warm by exerting ourselves. The problem was, we never had any steady exercise. We were either exercising violently for a short burst, or stuck and frozen.

At times during this period, Fritz felt very ill. The symptoms were strangely similar to those we had experienced during the worst period of the training programme when Roger, Allan and I would wake up with splitting headaches, feeling dizzy and sick, and even drunk at times. We would want to sit down every five minutes and rest. Possibly it was a form of carbon monoxide poisoning. On this trip, Fritz had exactly the same symptoms, but surprisingly Ken didn't get them although he was sharing a tent with Fritz at the time, nor did Allan or I. We never did get a satisfactory answer to this, although it was suggested that perhaps thoroughbred athletes are a little more vulnerable than cart-horses. Fritz's sickness coincided with some of the hardest sledging of the whole journey, when he was doing about two-thirds of the leading.

The cold was really nagging. It would cut right into one. We were often desperately hungry and very thirsty, but we couldn't stop at mid-day to put up a tent because we needed to go as fast as we could. From about eight o'clock in the morning till about eight or nine o'clock at night, we had no warm food or drink, and at the end of a hard day's sledging we would just collapse into our sleeping-bags and fall asleep.

However, the weather gradually improved, and as the sun came back we were able to put in longer and longer days. Fortunately the surface was improving, too. We found for the first time during the journey that we were consistently travelling across hard wind-packed snow. We were seeing 'sastrugi' for only about the second time during the journey. Sastrugi results from the effect of wind which will pack the snow down and polish it – and then start chiselling until there are waves in the snow, cut and chiselled by the wind. The sastrugi were not quite as regular as a ploughed field; they were like smooth waves, chiselled a little bit, and were a perfect surface for walking or running on. The sledges hardly left a track at all. If you were following another sledge, you would have to look hard to see just where it had cut through the top of the snow-wave or sastrugi, or to see the claw marks of the dogs where they had scratched the surface. There were no other signs at all – you couldn't see a man's footprint because we were usually wearing soft-soled shoes which left no impression.

The sledging procedure we were using at that time was based on the previous season's experience. Fritz and I would be first and second, Allan would be third, and Ken would come up last. The reason was that Fritz and I had worked together the previous year; and Allan, whose back was still suspect, needed someone there behind him to help if he got into difficulties. Now Allan had promised that he would never lift or heave anything, that he would always wait till we came up and gave him a hand. But you could quite often see him on the horizon struggling and heaving and tugging at the sledge, and then you'd go up to him and give him a ticking off and say 'Why didn't you wait for me, I was only five minutes away?' Sheepishly he would tell me that he was managing all right, that he had developed a technique of shoving and pushing, that he didn't feel any pain and was quite sure it wasn't doing any damage to his back. In fact, he never had the slightest hint of a twinge. Even his knee trouble, which he had had for years, didn't recur during that part of the journey. On the Greenland trip all three of us had suffered from sprains, twists and knee trouble. I remember being at the back of the column and seeing the other two limping. I was limping as well. All three of us were going along like old men. And even in the first part of the trans-Arctic journey, it was the same. All four of us were at one time limping.

We passed latitude 88°. The sun was back by this time and Venus had almost disappeared. The moon was there, but low in the sky, and the weather was warming up to about minus 35° to 40° Fahrenheit. We were progressing well across a good surface. The floes were sound and I began to think for the first time since Allan's accident that there was a chance we might get him all the way to Spitzbergen. After all, we'd come through the hardest and coldest part of the journey.

We were averaging only two miles a day to start with, but as the days grew longer we went on to the forced-marching routine. I sent a message back to Max Brewer suggesting that, instead of bringing the Cessna out from T-3 to the 88th or

89th parallel, why not wait until we got to the Pole? It is not often that Cessnas land at the North Pole. It would be tremendous publicity for the work and skill of the N.A.R.L. pilots; and if he was going to come out all that way, why come and pick Allan up at, say, 89° N which was only sixty nautical miles from the Pole? It would only take another twenty minutes of flying time to be at the Pole itself. Max Brewer agreed.

It had never been my intention at any time to by-pass the Pole on the Greenland side. That would have been the shortest possible route from our winter quarters to Spitzbergen. But the most favourable current, in fact, starts on the Siberian side of the dateline, passes the Pole and goes into the Greenland Sea, so we had to get to the Pole in order to pick up the most favourable drift. In other words, if we were going to make a detour round the Pole, it had to be on the eastern, the Russian side, rather than on the Canadian side. From leaving winter quarters, I was determined we should go to the Pole in any event. Bypassing it on the Canadian side would have put us too close to the Greenland Sea which we were trying to avoid. This was the real danger spot in the whole Arctic Ocean: it is the exit point for about eighty per cent of the ice of the Arctic Ocean which, as it gets closer to the Greenland Sea, moves faster and spews out into the North Atlantic.

Just before leaving winter quarters we had been told that Hugh Simpson, with his wife and Roger Tufft, was about to attempt an expedition to the North Pole from Canada, but we didn't know what date he was setting out, what weight he was carrying on his sledges, or when he planned to be at the Pole. As Freddie sent through more information, it did seem to us that we were going to have to hurry if we were to beat my old sledging companions. Admittedly they were starting quite a bit to the south of us, but we could easily have run into some kind of delaying problem. Allan might have had a relapse, for instance, or we might have got stuck in pressure ice.

For the first few days of the journey we had only been averaging two miles a day. All Hugh had to do was to average about ten miles a day and they would overhaul us. So although we couldn't really believe that he would beat us to the Pole – and in any case, we had to go as fast as we possibly could to reach Spitzbergen by mid-summer – we found the prospect of being beaten an added incentive to travel even harder. We probably put in about an extra half hour of travelling each day, more than we might otherwise have done. Somehow, not knowing where Hugh was or how fast he was going, made us feel tense. But then, as we climbed to within only sixty nautical miles of the Pole, word came through that he was having a hard struggle in the pressure ice off Ellesmere Island and had only progressed twenty-seven miles from the coast. We felt very sympathetic. We had had a similar experience ourselves after leaving Barrow in the early days, trying to get on to the polar pack.

From latitude 89° to the Pole was really invigorating. It seemed only a question of time and hard work. We had had our first R.C.A.F. airdrop of the season and the extras they dropped us, including steaks, eggs and beer, enabled us to eat like lords for the next couple of days. We must have been putting away 7,000 calories a day. The R.C.A.F. aircrew always gave us a few words of encouragement when they flew over, and told us what the going was like ahead. On that occasion they said it was not too good. As we got into the territory which they had been describing, however, we found that it was passable. The relief was like a shot in the arm – though there was always the possibility that the bad stuff was still farther ahead. There was always this thought that at any time we were going to run into impassable ice, that we'd be stopped or slowed down – but, in fact, it never happened. Conditions got better and better all the time. The surface was so good that once or twice the dogs actually broke into a gallop, the first time they had done so during the whole journey.

After about the halfway point from winter quarters to the Pole, we began to find that the floes weren't as broken up. They were holding together better but there were vast areas of thin ice, and some of these were the biggest frozen leads we had seen on the journey. Some were over a mile across. It just looked as though the whole of the Arctic Ocean had opened up and had then frozen over about a week or two earlier.

During the early weeks of the journey, we had been worried about travelling on six inches of sea ice which, with two blows of an ice axe, would go through. Later on, we took this thin ice in our stride. When temperatures are minus 30° to 40° Fahrenheit, even as you're sledging the ice is thickening up. It is so cold that the ice is probably about an eighth of an inch thicker by the time you have got across a quarter-mile-wide lead than it was when you started. The only snag with these really flat stretches was that the frozen sea ice was a bit sticky. It hadn't had time to get a cover of snow on it, hadn't had time for any of the salt to be drawn off by evaporation. We didn't in fact go any faster on these flat areas, but at least they provided smooth going. On the far side we would run up on to the bank and think that this was the last of the flat stretch. But then we'd find that, although back on the floes where the going was rougher, we actually went faster because the snow was really hard packed and the sledges just skidded over it. With the broader runners on our sledges we could avoid obstacles by just giving the sledge a push, and the whole thing would skid across the snow like a skier. The previous season we had never been able to do this; the sledge would bite in and 'track', and we would have to do three-point turns to get around obstacles. There were times on the best, hard surfaces when you could actually spin the sledge through 180 degrees.

As we drew nearer the Pole there were not only these vast areas of open water which had frozen over to a depth of five or six inches – there were no major pressure ridges either. There were more pressure ridges to the mile, but they were smaller. Sometimes we would go for days without having to chop through a pressure ridge of any size. We would just run the dogs at a pressure ridge, beat the traces, trundle over and thump down on to a young floe on the other side. It was exhilarating. We were on the move. Nothing now was going to stop us reaching the Pole.

11 On Top of the World

THE FIRST ATTEMPT TO MAKE A SURFACE CROSSING OF THE ARCTIC OCEAN WAS MADE BY A YOUNG NORWEGIAN, Bjørn Staib in 1964. His previous polar experience was limited. He had crossed the Greenland Ice Cap with dog teams a couple of years before and had driven dogs in the Norwegian mountains, but this was his first encounter with pack ice. He was obliged to organize his venture in a hurry and had more than his share of bad luck. He penetrated the Arctic pack ice and reached Arlis-2, an American scientific drifting station which at that time was almost midway between Northern Ellesmere Island and the Pole, and was moving rapidly towards the Greenland Sea. When Staib arrived at Arlis-2 to pick up supplies, the summer was already too far advanced and he had to abandon his attempt and fly out.

The next attempt at the Pole was by Ralph Plaisted, an insurance broker from Minnesota. His party travelled with motorized sledges – vehicles which are very popular among sportsmen in Canada and the northern United States. A fairly small vehicle it may be, but undoubtedly it has proved itself. Pulling a full load its speed is about the same as a dog team, and it can pull about the same weight. Its advantage over a dog team is that it can easily be unhitched from its sledge and used as a reconnaissance vehicle. On the other hand, with any kind of motorized vehicle, you only need one small part to go wrong, and if there are no spare parts available then that engine is out of action. With a dog team, if you lose one dog you have lost only one-ninth of the power.

I first met Plaisted at Eureka when I was halfway through the training programme for the trans-Arctic journey. We had travelled by that time about seven hundred miles and called at Eureka to resupply and to have a short rest before carrying on. His first attempt at the Pole by Skidoos had just failed, and he was returning via Eureka on his way south. He was a friendly and generous man with whom we got on well, so to me it was very satisfying that when he attempted it the second time he was successful. He reached the North Pole in April 1968, during the first summer of our journey across the Arctic Ocean, and from there he was flown out by Weldy Phipps in his twin-engined Otter. If neither Cook nor Peary were successful (and the claims of both are disputed), then Plaisted's achievement is so much the greater. Either way it was a relief to me, for I regard it as fitting in view of the Cook-Peary polar controversy that ultimately an American should get there first.

Plaisted's achievement does not, I feel, detract from our efforts because we had come to the North Pole by the longest axis. We had already covered more than twice the distance that Plaisted covered in reaching the Pole, and were going on beyond the Pole to make the first surface crossing of the Arctic Ocean. We were, therefore, in effect making a pioneer journey, whereas Plaisted's was a pioneer journey only in so far as he was using vehicles instead of the conventional sledges and dogs. We sent him our sincere congratulations, and now were shortly to be on the receiving end of congratulations ourselves.

Navigating by dead reckoning on the Arctic Ocean is complicated by the fact that the ice is drifting, and if you see no sun for several days you really have no exact idea where you might be. You know roughly in which direction you are going, but you don't know which way the ice is drifting; you don't know exactly how far you've travelled, because you have had to make so many detours. In the Antarctic where you're travelling across fairly flat, featureless country, you can tow along a sledge wheel which ticks off the distance in miles you've travelled. You cannot do this across the ice pack of the Arctic Ocean; the wheel would buckle before it had recorded ten miles, so you have no choice but to guess. Usually the guesses were quite good. We compared each other's guesses of the distance at the end of the day and it was seldom that our guesses were more than a mile from the mean. Our final approach to the Pole was made on dead-reckoning using a very hazy sun for a general direction.

On the 5th April we pitched our camp feeling sure that we must be within two miles of the Pole. Overnight a blizzard blew up which obscured the sun altogether; there was no chance of a fix. In the very early hours of the morning, however, the wind died down, the sky cleared, the sun came out and every couple of hours I'd go outside and do a sun shot. I could not compute these fixes – Allan had all the tables in his tent and I didn't want to wake him up. I felt in any case that there would be time enough later that morning to confirm the position, and sent out by radio the following message to Her Majesty the Queen:

I have the honour to inform your Majesty that today, 5th April, at 0700 hours Greenwich Mean Time, the British Trans-Arctic Expedition by dead reckoning reached the North Pole 407 days after setting out from Point Barrow, Alaska. My companions of the crossing party, Allan Gill, Major Kenneth Hedges, R.A.M.C., and Dr Roy Koerner, together with Squadron Leader Church, R.A.F., our radio relay officer at Point Barrow, are in good health and spirits and hopeful that by forced marches and a measure of good fortune the Expedition will reach Spitzbergen by Mid-summer's Day of this year, thus concluding in the name of our Country the first surface crossing of the Arctic Ocean. (Signed W. W. Herbert, Expedition Leader.)

Allan came across with the computed position just after I had finished transmitting and had switched off the radio. I was shaken to find that we were seven miles short of the Pole, instead of only about a mile and a half. Feeling that one ought to be at least within two miles of the Pole before saying that by dead reckoning one has reached it, we packed up immediately, broke camp and got going to try and put ourselves where we had said we were. It was about 9 a.m. We had several hours to go before the G.M.T. date changed, and there was a pretty good chance that in that time we'd get to the Pole.

Navigation in the vicinity of the Pole is a problem. If your calculation of the longitude is slightly out, then the time at which the sun crosses your meridian – in other words that time at which the sun is due north – is wrong, and so you head in the wrong direction. And of course, if you head in the wrong direction, you increase your errors in your dead reckoning longitude. Your azimuth then is thrown even further into error and you increase your errors progressively until you spiral into almost a complete circle. This is what happened to us on this particular day.

We set off and travelled for what we estimated was seven miles and stopped. We set up the theodolite, did a rough calculation, and found that we were still seven miles from the Pole. It was unbelievable. We had used up a lot of our time in getting there – the G.M.T. date was going to change within the next seven hours and we were still seven miles short of our goal. We couldn't understand where we had gone wrong. How could one travel seven miles in the direction of the North Pole and still be seven miles from it? The only possible answer was that we must have been travelling parallel to the dateline and were thus passing the Pole. We concluded there must have been something very wrong with our azimuth taken from the position we had computed that morning; so we went into the computations again, and found an error in the longitude. We did another series of observations, all of which took time, and set off again. We travelled hard for three hours, set up a theodolite yet again, and found that we were three miles south of the Pole and on longitude zero. With Spitzbergen as our goal and being still three weeks behind schedule, we should really have carried straight on and not gone back.

But one cannot with a clear conscience say one is at the Pole when one is three miles short of it – more especially since we had told Her Majesty that by dead reckoning we had reached it. So we set off yet again, travelling on a very precise azimuth. We chopped through every single pressure ridge that came our way, cutting ourselves a dead straight line due north. But it was slow progress and the drift was going against us. We were, in fact, hardly making any progress at all. After about four hours we'd come less than a mile.

In desperation, we off-loaded the sledges, laid a depot and took on with us only the barest essentials, just enough for one night's camp. It was a risk, the only time during the whole journey that we took such a risk. But it paid off. With the lighter sledges we made faster progress, and after about three hours estimated that we must surely be at the Pole, possibly even beyond it. So we stopped, set up our tents, and did a final fix which put us at 89°59' N, one mile south of the North Pole on longitude 180. In other words, we'd crossed the Pole about a mile back along our tracks. But the drift was now with us, so we must surely cross the Pole a second time as we drifted overnight. We got into our sleeping-bags and fell asleep.

The pad marks of thirty-five Eskimo huskies, the broad tracks of four heavy Eskimo-type sledges, and the four sets of human footprints which had approached the North Pole and halted one mile beyond it on the morning of Easter Sunday, 1969, no longer mark the spot where we took our final sun shots and snatched a few hours' rest. For even while we were sleeping, our camp was slowly drifting; and the Pole, by the time we had reloaded our sledges a few hours later and set course for the island of Spitzbergen, lay north in a different direction.

It had been an elusive spot to find and fix. At the North Pole, two separate sets of meridians meet and all directions are south. The temperature was minus 35° Fahrenheit. The wind was from the south-west, or was it from the north-east? It was Sunday, or was it Saturday? Maybe it was Monday. It was a confusing place to be – a place which lay on our course from Barrow to Spitzbergen and which had taken us 408 days to reach.

Trying to set foot upon it had been like trying to step on the shadow of a bird that was circling overhead. The surface across which we were moving was itself a moving surface on a planet that was spinning about an axis. We were standing approximately on that axis, asleep on our feet, dog tired and hungry. Too tired to celebrate our arrival on the summit of this super-mountain around which the sun circles almost as though stuck in a groove.

We set up our camera and posed for some pictures – thirty-six shots at different exposures. We tried not to look weary, tried not to look cold. We tried only to huddle, four fur-clad figures, in a pose that was vaguely familiar – for what other proof of the attainment could we bring back than a picture posed in this way?

12 Towards the Land

ON THE 8TH APRIL WE WERE MORE THAN 2° LATITUDE BEHIND SCHEDULE, HAVING ONLY SIXTY DAYS LEFT IN which to cover an absolute minimum of six hundred nautical miles. Men and dogs were broken down as a result of the gruelling sledging of the last six weeks in temperatures of minus 40° to 50° Fahrenheit, on a well-balanced but insufficient diet of 5,000 calories a day. We could not, I told the Committee in a radio message of that date, possibly maintain the necessary average of twelve to fourteen nautical miles per day unless we could arrange to receive on each of the next two R.C.A.F. airdrops five hundred pounds of red meat for the dogs; supplementary rations for the men to increase their calorie intake to approximately 6,000 calories a day; and unless we could lighten the loads of all non-essential gear, and keep moving.

My message continued:

Arrangements are in hand to cover the red meat for the dogs and the supplementary rations for the men and I intend, in view of the great distance we are from T-3 and the many logistic problems Dr Brewer is at present faced with in support of that station, to jettison all non-essential instruments and gear and proceed to Spitzbergen with Gill in company. We will of course not, repeat, not jettison film or scientific records.

I doubt if this message came as a surprise to the Committee or, for that matter, the letter I sent to Max Brewer of the same date; both of them must have realized that my greatest dilemma was how to get rid of the exposed film, instruments and scientific records without getting rid of Allan.

. . . Max, it is with the very deepest sense of gratitude that I recognize your offer made some time ago to assist this Expedition by sending out two Cessnas with R4D cover to relieve us of our scientific instruments, exposed film and records. However, in view of your many logistic problems in supporting T-3 and the great distance we expect to be from that station by the 16th April (450 nautical miles), the urgency with which we must press for Spitzbergen, and the relatively small pay-load of film and instruments that would be collected from us (the Lamont equipment was left at winter quarters on the authorisation of Dr Hunkins), I feel that the complex and costly operation of sending out two Cessnas with R4D cover is no longer justified. It will of course be a great disappointment to Geoff Renner who has so patiently and sympathetically held himself in readiness at Barrow to join us as a replacement for Allan. Geoff has followed our progress with great interest and no doubt a little envy as we struggled those last few miles to the Pole. . . .

For the first time since his accident the previous September, Allan breathed a sigh of relief. He never at any time regarded the possibility of a relapse with the seriousness of a man who wants an excuse or sympathy. He worked very hard on the exercises designed for him by Ken during the winter, and in his own rather peculiar way, he took care not to put any undue strain on his back.

Of course there are plenty of other ways of making life difficult for yourself on the Arctic Ocean besides slipping a disc – you can, for example, burn down your tent. It is easily done. Indeed, I am surprised it is not done more often. All you have to do is go outside, as Allan did on the first day south of the

Pole on the homeward side, to test the balance of a dog whip
he had just finished making; Fritz was already outside drilling
a hole through the ice to measure its thickness. Who actually
spotted smoke pouring from the apex of the tent I cannot
recall, but with a bit of quick action they were able to save one
or two items of clothing, and by working through to 2 p.m.
(we were on a routine of night travel and twelve hours out of
phase), they were able to patch the tent well enough to keep
out all but the sharpest of breezes.

On the 9th April at latitude 89°17′ N, longitude 09°00′ E,
we were spotted by a U.S. Airforce weather reconnaissance
aircraft. They had come up on our frequency when at about
latitude 88° N on the Barrow side of the Pole, and asked if we
had any smoke flares. 'I can do better than that,' I told them.
'I'll switch on the Elliott homing beacon.' We had a very
pleasant chat – which cost us an extra hour's work on the hand
generator – and was surprised and delighted to hear that Colonel
Joe Fletcher was on board. The American drifting station T-3,
otherwise known as Fletcher's Ice Island, is named after him;
he was the first pilot to spot and to land on the ice island in
1952. 'I was very impressed by what I heard over the radio,'
he said later, on landing at the U.S. Air base at Mildenhall in
England. 'They are obviously very competent and very pro-
fessional in their approach to their task. They are well organized and extremely healthy, and their radio technique was
impeccable.'

Among the many topics of mutual interest we discussed, as
they were homing in on us and droning overheard, was their
flight track. I learnt with interest that the weather aircraft flies
the route once a day – from Europe to Alaska via the North
Pole one day, and returning along the same track the next.
From the Pole they fly down the thirtieth meridian east until
clear of the Arctic Ocean, and their E.T.A. at the Pole is
generally within a few minutes of the same time every day.
This set me thinking. With the poor radio propogation we

were experiencing at that time, and the prospect of more difficult radio conditions as we increased our distance from Freddie, it would be prudent to come to some arrangement with the U.S. Airforce.

I did not work out the details for several days, for the subject of which route to take in our approach to Spitzbergen required very careful thought and a lot more information before I would commit the party. Meanwhile, we changed course slightly and moved over to longitude 30° E, which at that latitude was no great distance. We found it more convenient from the navigational point of view to choose a longitude and stick to it, and over the next few days I sent out several messages seeking the predictions and latest weather and ice reports for the north shore of Spitzbergen. I had, of course, made a very detailed study of the ice conditions in the Spitzbergen area many years ago as part of the basic plan; but ice conditions vary considerably from one year to the next, indeed from week to week at that time in the year when the ice starts to loosen up. I also came to an unofficial arrangement with a weather reconnaissance crew to call them up on the radio every second day and get from them a 'bird's-eye' description of the ice conditions immediately to our north, and over a distance of sixty nautical miles directly to our south. The aircrews being unfamiliar with ice conditions which we regarded as easy or troublesome, it was more useful to us to have a purely comparative description of the ice conditions they would see from their window, and this way we could judge for ourselves how the going ahead would compare with what we had already crossed.

From these regular flights along our route, from the flights of the U.S. Navy ice reconnaissance, from weather satellite information supplied by the U.S. Oceanographic office, and from the predictions of specialists in the subject of ice concentration and movement, I decided on an approach to Spitzbergen along a track that would take us parallel to the major leads, give us a respectable margin of safety in case we were halted by the conditions or by injury in the closing stages, and bring us to a landfall on the northernmost off-shore islands, the Sjöuyane group – a group twenty-odd miles from an un-occupied but well-stocked Norwegian hut at Depottoden on North East Land. I then informed Freddie and the Committee that, in the event of radio failure, we would activate our homing beacon from 0700 to 0705 hours G.M.T. every day; that we would proceed down longitude 30° E as far as latitude 83° N, where we would alter course, head directly for Phipps Island, and make a landfall on or about the 3rd June. I had pro-vided Freddie and the Committee with a revised set of target dates, one for every degree through to the landfall, and sent a letter to the Chief Defence Staff at Canadian Headquarters in Ottawa in which I laid out a contingency plan. In fifteen travelling days since leaving the Pole we had sledged about 220 nautical miles and made good three degrees of latitude. Given the same travelling condition over the next fifteen days, it would not be unreasonable to expect that we would be at latitude 84° N by the next and last scheduled R.C.A.F. re-supply drop on the 10th May, and continuing at this same rate of progress, we would make our landfall on the north coast of Spitzbergen on schedule about the 4th June:

We intend making every possible effort to reach this target, but in spite of the favourable drift of ice from which we hope to benefit during the final two hundred nautical miles of our journey, it would be unrealistic to expect travelling con-ditions to remain as good throughout the month of May as they were in early April; indeed, reports from the U.S. weather aircraft flying daily along meridian 30° E indicate that the ice conditions deteriorate south of latitude 86° N, and reports from Norwegian sources state that the pack ice is badly broken off the north coast of Spitzbergen.

It is essential therefore that a contingency plan is laid. The plan calls for an airdrop on or about the 4th June which would equip us with light-weight man-hauling sledges and an inflatable rubber boat, and food and fuel enough to keep us going for about thirty days. Details I will transmit in a separate message via Sir Vivian Fuchs and your Air Attaché's office in London. May it suffice here to say that I am confident with one additional airdrop we would meet the contingency and make our landfall and our rendezvous with H.M.S. *Endurance* safely about Midsummer's Day.

It is my wish, as I am sure it is the wish also of the R.C.A.F., that No. 435 Squadron make this additional airdrop; for that squadron, having so expertly and enthusiastically supported the Expedition throughout the crossing would, I am sure, regard their support as incomplete and their achievement like ours as having fallen short of the goal should we fail to reach our destination.

The ice conditions we were meeting during that period cannot be judged by the rate of progress unless one considers the many psychological factors which influenced this journey. We had, by this stage, had more sledging experience on the Arctic Ocean than any of our predecessors. We had spent fourteen months on the ice pack and grown accustomed to the sights, sounds, and movement of ice. We had survived four seasons and, in spite of the many setbacks and frustrations, had reached the North Pole by the longest axis and received many messages of congratulation which, although in a sense premature, were, nevertheless, a tremendous incentive to push on and complete the journey. The weather was getting warmer, we could work the dogs more comfortably, and could put in more hours before we ploughed through misery towards a target time set each morning whilst we were still warm and eager. But with each degree that the temperature rose, and with each sign that indicated the advance of the season, there grew an anxiety which only miles and more miles could alleviate. It had become a race with the season, a race in which we were handicapped out of all reason, and which we could only win by driving ourselves and our dogs to the limit of our physical endurance. We made progress by working for it across country where good progress was possible only for men with a greater incentive than the enticing hope of success – we made miles to save our skins.

For six days we had been without radio contact when, on the morning of the 16th April, I switched on the radio in the hope of contacting the R.C.A.F. Hercules which was scheduled on that date to make a supply drop. We had, on that day, one day's supply of food and fuel left. The Captain of the Hercules and Tony Dawe of *The Sunday Times* were well aware of this:

. . . They had camped on ice eighty miles from their last known position south of the Pole. They were hoping desperately that the aircraft would find them, only too aware of the fate ahead if they were lost on the ice without food and fuel. The strain showed in Herbert's voice as I listened to him over the radio aboard the Hercules. His voice was flat, drained by the tension, but slowly relief flooded through and I heard the more familiar cheerful tones. He said, 'We are so relieved to hear you. We have been out of radio contact and quite honestly we didn't expect to hear the aircraft.' Captain Ronning and his crew from the Canadian Airforce 435 Squadron at Edmonton shared Wally's delight and relief. They had set out from the American base at Thule on Greenland's north-west coast on a seemingly impossible mission. Radio conditions were atrocious, and without contact with the Expedition they would have to search hundreds of miles of ice looking for the tiny figures of men and the huskies amid the confusing shadows. For forty minutes we had searched an area between the 88 and 89th parallels before Herbert's voice suddenly came up on the radio to tell us that his position was 88° north 30° east. Captain Ronning requested the weather conditions and Herbert replied 'Just

stand by . . . I'll stick my head out of the tent. . . .' A few
seconds later: 'Clear blue sky and dead calm'. The Expedition
lit a marker flare and suddenly we saw a red spot about seven
miles away on the ice. As we approached we could clearly
see the red smoke like a smudge on a white-washed wall,
the first true colour we had seen in three hours of flying over
the Arctic. The Hercules descended to 350 ft for the first
drop. The loading doors opened and the crew listened to a
countdown from the flightdeck, 'five, four, three, two,
one . . .' the last strap restraining the carefully packed tent
was cut . . . 'zero'. . . . When the men unpacked the tent
they found inside a 'No Smoking' sign – put there by the
men from C.A.F. Air Despatch School at Rivers, Manitoba,
who had repaired the tent which had been used by the
Expedition on their Greenland Training programme. The
tent would replace the one burnt out one day south of the
Pole. The next two drops included the routine supplies,
twenty-three boxes of dog food, five boxes of men rations,
twenty-four gallons of fuel, stoves, ice axes, and some extras
specially packed by the Air Despatch School – twelve
steaks, twenty-four cans of beer, fresh fruit. The Hercules
then climbed to 900 ft for the last drop – a new sledge to
replace one battered by the rough ice the Expedition had
encountered on its journey to the North Pole. Ahead of the
Expedition the ice was jagged. A range of pressure ridges
stretched about half a mile presenting them with a major
obstacle. They would have to hack a twisting path wide
enough for the sledges to get through the rough ice – still an
exhausting task in temperatures around minus 20°F. As we
flew on, Captain Ronning quoted the ice conditions: 'I hate
to say it but the ice seems pretty rough for the next fifty to a
hundred miles.' Herbert replied: 'That's bad news.' The
better ice conditions the party have experienced since the
Pole are obviously at an end. They have travelled one
hundred and forty miles from the Pole in less than a fortnight

and are now about six hundred statute miles from Spitzbergen, which they hope to reach by mid-June before the ice
breaks up. Herbert told me, 'Since we left the Pole we have
been held up by nothing until we stopped last night to
prepare for the airdrop. We decided the best thing to do
when we had lost radio contact was to press on and travel
hard. We have been putting in twelve hours outside the tent
and travelling for ten of them. We ought to continue this
hard travelling to keep to our schedule. We ought to make
five degrees (345 statute miles) before the next airdrop in
twenty-five days' time. From the sound of the ice conditions ahead, it will be a hard task.' We wished him Good
Luck before we flew out of range. They are probably the
last words he will hear from the outside world for several
days until radio conditions improve.

A slightly less informed article had appeared in *Newsweek* on
the 21st April:

Sometime this week, the Royal Air Force will attempt to
air drop a new tent and other supplies to the beleagured
Expedition. There is already speculation in London that the
Royal Air Force will also be called upon before long to
evacuate the entire Expedition but 34-year-old Wally
Herbert, the team's Leader and a dedicated explorer, still
insists that he and his men can finish the course ahead of their
implacable deadline. 'It will be a bit uncomfortable,' he
admits with the understated calm so vital to his lonely job,
'but we shall manage somehow.'

On the 26th April we ran into an area of violent ice movement, and came closer than at any time during the journey to
losing a sledge and a team of dogs. Allan was at that time in the
lead. He and Fritz had hacked through a pressure ridge on to a
strip of rubble and mush ice which, although wet, was quiet.

There was another ridge on the far side of the strip of mush which, at the moment Allan set foot upon it, started to groan. I went over with him and gave him a hand negotiating the ridge on the far side, but we had no sooner got the dogs safely on to the far bank than the mush ice started to 'boil' and the floe on which we were standing to tilt up to an angle of 30°. An immediate choice had to be made between my sledge and Allan's. Mine carried a radio, Allan's geophysical records, a duplicate set of Fritz's records, one or two sets of navigational gear (the other set was on Allan's sledge), tables, the theodolite, and half the exposed and unexposed film stock. We decided to abandon Allan's sledge and cut his dogs loose, whilst I scrambled back across the bucking slippery blocks and mush to save my own team. The whole floe was splitting up and moving. With some frantic manœuvres, Ken, Fritz and I managed to get our three teams away from the immediate danger and leapt across several fractures to a slightly bigger floe. Allan, left on his own, meanwhile discovered that he was cut off from the floe beyond by a fissure in the ice; it was some fourteen feet deep and the bottom was of compacted slush. I went back to give him a hand while Ken and Fritz looked around for an alternative route by which the four of us could reunite. The mush ice was in constant movement. Several times I was about to set foot on the crossing when it would suddenly boil up: green blocks the size of bungalows would rise out of the stew of ice débris and collapse with a dull thud back into the mush. We got out of that spot with dog power and sweat; and by a detour of over a mile across the fractured floes, eventually found a way on to the safer country to our south.

The leads and fractures by this time were becoming a problem, and many long diversions were necessary to make any progress south. It was by now taking many days for newly-opened leads to freeze over. There were many indications that the summer was coming early – thin ice on the larger leads were darkening and becoming soft. The sledges broke through to slop several times a day, but it was about this time nevertheless that we put in our best mileages, for the country kept rolling ahead of us and every minor obstacle kept opening the way to more floes and minor detours. We made twenty-three nautical miles on the 2nd May. In route miles that day we covered at least twenty-seven nautical miles, putting us at the end of the day at latitude 84°53' N, longitude 31·1° E. We were putting in sometimes as much as twelve hours of sledging and at the end of each day were dead tired and very hungry.

By the 10th May we were at latitude 83° N – the point on our course at which we were to turn and head for land. On that same day we received what was to have been our last air drop from the 435 Squadron R.C.A.F. – a brilliantly executed mission. At an altitude of 15,000 feet they picked up our beacon at a range of 50 miles but lost it on their descent, and, as usual, we brought them in by listening for the sound of the engines and passing them directions over the radio. They descended to 250 feet in fog and, roaring over us, despatched their load in two passes. We could not have seen the aircraft for more than five seconds of each pass. The Captain of the aircraft caught only a split-second glance at his target, but the 'chutes all landed within one hundred yards of the dropping zone. There were fogs from then on almost every day, but this was to be expected, for on the Arctic Ocean May is the month of mists. One staggers forward in a white blindfold, stumbling into pits one cannot see, across pans of ice that seem at first as limitless as oceans on a compass course past misty shapes which grow, then shrink, and fade away.

Rising at 1500 hours, we would travel through the night and sleep outside on the sledges during the heat of the day when the temperature rose to about 20° Fahrenheit. By the 22nd May the ice was getting slushy, and for the first time since the summer of 1968 we could smell the sea. Wild life suddenly became abundant. In the last three days we had seen a total of forty-three birds of six different species, come upon fresh tracks of polar bear, sighted seals and a school of six narwhals. This co-location of wild life was perhaps to be expected for we were by then only fifty miles from the nearest land, and must therefore have crossed the 100-fathom line.

With a good day's travel on the following day we expected to be within sight of Phipps Island – fifteen months to the day since we lost sight of Point Barrow, Alaska, on the other side of the Arctic Ocean. Had we made the right approach?

South of latitude 83° N, dark reflections on the cloud base, like a full-scale map, had indicated all the major leads within ten miles of our position. We had run parallel to the principal waterways, and were obliged to cross only the smaller fractures which linked them. We would have been very foolish to have approached Spitzbergen any other way, for what we could not see for ourselves reflected on the clouds was confirmed when the cloud cover occasionally broke, and the satellites looked down on the break-up of the ice.

13 Landfall

W E SIGHTED LAND ON THE 23RD MAY. IT HAD BEEN A
PERFECT DAY WITH NOT A CLOUD IN THE SKY EXCEPT
those clouds on the horizon in the direction of land. It was also
the first day we were bothered by polar bears. A couple of
polar bears came up behind us whilst we were sledging and
were effectively shooed away. But from then onwards we
encountered polar bears all the way to the landfall. They were
becoming a menace. Every day we saw at least two, and we
were also meeting at that time a lot more broken ice than we
had met previously. The floes were pretty cracked up with the
pressure building up. The surface was also getting bad by that
time and there was quite a lot of slush around. So it was almost
touch and go whether we were going to get on to land anyway.
The sledging season was quickly ending and we were journey-
ing then as fast as we possibly could. But we were only making
about eight to ten miles a day.

The land was taking a long time to get closer and there were
many white-outs. When the weather cleared we always expected to see the land much closer, but it seemed just as far
away. We seemed to be travelling and travelling but making
no progress. The distraction, however, was the polar bears and
we killed three during those three days. Sometimes they would
come down-wind, but usually they approached us from behind
and they just kept coming. There was one occasion when a
polar bear came in sight and Fritz was in an awkward position:
he was trying to cross a stretch of very tricky ice, weak, sloppy
ice, with rotten small pans of ice in the middle of it, and

suddenly a polar bear came along. The dogs of course took off and dragged the sledge into the water. The sledge didn't go right down but it rocked into the water. It was pulled out with a great deal of difficulty. And all this time the polar bear kept on coming, and Fritz didn't know what to do: whether to shoot it with a gun, shoot it with a camera, or try and rescue the sledge. All the other dog teams were going berserk and it was absolute chaos. We had only three guns, so one of us had no means of self-defence, myself on this occasion. I had the camera with a telephoto lens and was taking pictures as fast as I could. But the polar bear was approaching the lead sledge from ahead, and Fritz and Ken were up by the dogs in front. Allan was just behind with his dogs, keeping them under control, and I was at the back taking pictures of the whole scene. Fritz and Ken fired a couple of shots, but it wouldn't go away. It just kept coming. It didn't actually attack – it just kept walking. You've got to shoot them sometimes otherwise they would come right on and hit you, and there is no way of knowing how close they will come before they turn round and walk away – if they do walk away at all.

To kill a polar bear, you had first to knock him over. We never went for a head shot in these situations. We would always have at least two guns aimed at him at the same time, or even three, and we didn't take any chances. This wasn't a sport, this was the real thing. We were killing to protect ourselves and the dogs, and also for dog food – but that was a very secondary motive because we had plenty of food at that time.

Polar bears normally travel on all fours. They will rise up on their hind legs occasionally, when they are some distance off, just to look over the pressure ridges. They are very fearsome but very beautiful, too. When they are some distance off, they are magnificent beasts, but when they come closer and closer, they do become very menacing. They just amble towards you with a completely fearless expression on their faces. Almost casually, they look over their shoulders and don't seem particularly interested in you at all, but they keep heading in your direction. They don't look you straight in the eye and come towards you; they casually close the distance. The previous summer a polar bear had come right in amongst the dogs and taken a few swipes at them. A couple of other times when they were heading for the dogs we had driven them off.

We couldn't take chances, and we dropped this particular one about fifteen feet away. That's as close as I want to be to a polar bear, and from that time on we decided that we would shoot all polar bears that came within twenty feet, though we always tried to scare them off. We tried several techniques. There was one occasion when all four of us, with three guns between us, walked towards the polar bear, making a lot of noise and shouting and so on. But he kept coming. As we were walking towards him, we were closing the distance that much quicker. It was ridiculous. We should really have been going the other way.

The polar bears seemed unused to humans and dogs. Most of them travel all over the ice cap but this was an area where they appeared to concentrate all along the coast of North-East Land. Probably most of the hunting is done in the summer off the north-west coast of Spitzbergen in the open water. But that is farther along the coast and there's pack ice round there and boats can't get that far.

It seemed a shame, having shot a polar bear, even in self-defence, to leave it there, so we felt obliged to chop it up for dog food. It took about a couple of hours and was very hard work for all four of us. But the dogs now began to associate the walking polar bear with the meat and, from that time on, it was impossible to hold them whenever a polar bear came in sight. They just went wild and were very difficult to control.

The following day, the 27th, we had a tremendous run first thing in the morning after an initial bad patch at the beginning when we were going across some very rough ice which cracked up. We then got on to some youngish ice and were making excellent progress alongside a lead. Polar bear tracks by this time were all over the place. There were literally hundreds and hundreds of tracks going in every direction. One could see the tracks approaching a lead and then the point at which they disappeared. A few minutes later the track would reappear from the lead with all the signs of where the bear had had a struggle to jump out.

Finally, after travelling for about four to five hours, we saw Phipps Island. It was a beautiful sight. The sky overhead was overcast, but to the south-east it was blue with superb lighting effects. The sunlight just rested on Phipps Island. Beyond, it was all blue sky.

All the ice between us and Phipps Island was a pale grey-blue colour, the sky a very dark greyish sepia with this superb colouring on Phipps Island. That was, I think, the most beautiful sight we had of Phipps Island. At that time we were struggling through some pretty rough ice, after the good stretch. Across one particularly difficult pressure ridge we could see the blood tracks where a polar bear had dragged a seal from a nearby lead. It had dragged it about fifty yards, and then pulled it over a pressure ridge which was about fifteen feet high, down the other side, and then finished it off. There were only just a few bones left, and as soon as the dogs picked up the tracks and followed the trail of blood, there was no stopping them. On the other side of the pressure ridge, we came on to another floe which stretched right to the horizon. There were no signs in the distance of any further pressure ridges – just Phipps Island in the radiant light.

We were now about seven miles from the island, and we'd put in a good four miles of perfect going, dead flat, across the floe. This made me think it might be landfast ice, and that without more difficulty we would make land that day. For the first time in the whole journey I thought we were definitely going to make it. Until you have actually set foot on land, you can never be absolutely sure because the ice is moving all the time, and anything may happen. Allan and Ken were way ahead. Allan was in the lead. His back hadn't played up at all and it seemed ridiculous to keep him always at No. 3 when he might as well go out ahead. I could barely see him in the distance and Ken was behind. Fritz and I were running parallel to each other, about twenty yards apart and just chatting. We had been doing this for about an hour, chatting as we were driving along, sitting on the sledge. And then we noticed that we were beginning to close on Allan and Ken. They were a good three or four miles from Phipps Island, and presumably had met some problem. They started to veer off to the right. As we closed up, we found out what it was. In that moment, we realized this was the end of the floe. We weren't going to get on to Phipps Island. Separating us from the island was an enormous stretch of water and broken-up mush ice. We had no choice but to run parallel or alongside the edge of the lead. We did this for about a couple of miles and eventually decided to turn into the mush ice and just take pot luck.

Allan about this time had had a nasty little scare with a polar bear. He normally never carried a gun. I only saw him on a couple of occasions with a gun in his hand, and that was usually when I was doing some filming. But on this occasion, he really had a shock. A polar bear suddenly appeared when he was a long way ahead of Ken, and all he had for protection was a parachute flare. The fact that he actually got one of the flares out of his bag and aimed it at the bear seems to suggest that he was not happy with the situation. In fact the polar bear did go away, which was surprising. If it had been aimed very accurately, the flare might have hit the polar bear and scared him off, but the chances are it would have made no difference.

That evening, after a long sledging day, Phipps Island seemed so close that we just felt we had to make an attempt to get on to it. We turned into the mush ice and had an extremely rough passage for about a mile and a half. I had one complete over-turn, a turn-turtle job where the sledge hit a piece of ice in an awkward direction, and neatly turned right over, landing in a melt pool upside down. All my moving cameras and film had been sitting right on the top of the sledge as this was obviously the safest place for them. I could afford to go into a melt pool down to about four feet deep without the box getting wet. It never occurred to me that I might turn-turtle with the box sitting in the water and the rest of the stuff completely dry. I had a hell of a job getting it out, but eventually, after tugging and yanking, we succeeded in righting the sledge. Luckily, the box containing the camera was sealed. We had taken the precaution of putting rubber around it on the inside for insulation.

That evening we found ourselves on a small floe, a pan of ice about 150 yards across, so we pitched camp, ate a meal and decided we would sleep out that night. We set up some stakes, some marker flags, and lined them up with certain features on Phipps Island to see how much we were moving in relation to it. And within about an hour of setting up camp on the floe, we found that we really were drifting at an alarming speed past Phipps Island. We were about a mile and a half, or two miles, from Phipps Island at the nearest point; but although we were closing on it very slightly, we were passing it by and drifting along. Overnight we drifted about six miles in a period of about eight hours, so we were really moving. This was alarming. Had we been going parallel to Phipps Island, it wouldn't have been so bad; but we were closing on it slightly, and there was a fair chance that we might bump up against the far corner of it. This, of course, would smash the floe to pieces.

The floes were about a couple of hundred yards across, and the mush ice was quite impossible to pass. We couldn't go back. We had to stay where we were. We didn't sleep too well over-night, and kept waking up. Every time I woke up, I would look out at Phipps Island, which seemed much closer. By this time the cliffs were towering up. We were about a quarter of a mile from the island by breakfast time, but moving very fast. With the naked eye, it really did look as if we were going to collide. We did a reconnaissance straight away to see if we could get off the floe but it was quite impossible. Everything was sloppy around us, and there was not a chance of moving on to any other of the pans of ice. For about five hours we just had to sit and wait, and see what would happen.

Now to the north-west of Phipps Island, about five miles away, there was a small island. We didn't know what it was called at that time but later learned that it was Little Blackboard Island. The general drift of the ice was between that island and Phipps Island. As the floe closed towards the divide between the two islands, we guessed that there might be a certain concentration of pack ice at that point. This was just a theory and so we said 'Okay, let's get ready'. The moment the floes all touched up as they jostled together, we would just go. This is exactly what happened, whether by coincidence or good judgement I shall never know. As soon as we were on a dead straight line between the two islands, the floes all bunched up to get through. Immediately, we moved off north-west towards Little Blackboard Island. By then it was obvious that we weren't going to get on to Phipps Island. We had already passed it, in fact. We had a reasonable chance of travelling towards Little Blackboard Island, but there were one or two very dicey spots as we soon found when we began to cross moving ice, some of which was very risky. But by this time, we had had great experience and we were all geared up to get on to land. Fritz and Ken were ahead. I stopped to load up a movie camera and got left behind. When I eventually caught Allan up, we found we were separated from the other two by a belt of mush ice; and the whole area, by this time, the morning of the 28th, was very sloppy. It took us about five hours to reunite with the other two and the operation was somewhat dangerous. The whole area was moving. For instance, we would reach a lead where there would be many pans of ice, but the whole thing would be gyrating. It would move in one direction to start with, shifting at about two knots; then it would stop and suddenly move back again at about one and a half knots, going backwards and forwards all the time.

We were then about three-quarters of a mile from Little Blackboard Island, at least Allan and I were. Fritz and Ken were on the other side of the lead. While we were waiting for the ice to settle down, they had gone off and tried to get on to land. Evidently they had got to within fifty yards of it. At that point was a lead which was being kept open by a tide race, and the loose ice in it was shifting, they reckoned, at about four knots. So this small gap of fifty yards, of course, was impassable. They waited there for quite a while hoping to get across. They reckoned that had they come a little earlier, they might just have got on to land. When they first arrived there, it was fairly quiet and they might, by leaping across from one piece of ice to the other, have landed, but it would have been very risky. They waited. They hesitated, and the whole area started to move, so they couldn't go. In many respects, it was just as well. They might have been stranded on the island.

Little Blackboard Island is a granite rock, about one thousand feet high, a spectacular rock from certain angles. When we first saw it, it didn't look very impressive, but from the angle at which we approached it, it was really a grand sight – a great tower, with very little scree, of granite rock. The cloud base was about eight hundred to nine hundred feet, so it was just chopping off the top of the island. It had very steep cliffs which looked dark in those lighting conditions. It was just a great, ferocious black rock going up into the clouds, but you knew that it wouldn't go much higher. In other words, the summit was already beginning to tail off, and the clouds just snipped it off at the top. The cloud at that height reflects all the water and so you have patches of black all over the clouds. You can see the land on the cloud base with all the water around you. Little

Blackboard Island was jet black, all the cloud above it was jet black, with the reflection off the rocks and the reflection off the water as well. It was an unforgettable sight; very sinister. It might only have been a quarter of a mile in diameter, but it was an island. No more, or less, of an island than Spitzbergen. If we were going to make a landing anywhere, we might just as well land there.

It could be argued, I suppose, that we were trying to get to Spitzbergen and that we had failed. But then Spitzbergen is also an island, and if you want to get on to the mainland, you have to go to Europe. So I felt that, providing we could get on to this outcrop, that was the end of the journey. But it did seem at the time quite impossible. Eventually, Allan and I took a chance on going across this lead and just bouncing from one piece of mush to another as it tightened up. It would tighten and hold for a second or two, and one had to time it precisely and just go. Then it would all slacken off again and start moving. We did finally manage to get across to rejoin Fritz and Ken, but we were all very depressed that night. I took some movies when we reunited, and looking now at the films one can see how obviously depressed we were.

Looking up at the rocks, we didn't think we were going to make it. The previous night we had drifted something like six or seven miles, and there was every reason to believe that we would do the same thing again – that we would drift away from the island in a north-westerly direction, and by the following morning, find ourselves five miles away – a perfectly reasonable assumption. So we set up camp that night, and I reported that we had got to within fifty yards of land, having got to within two hundred yards the previous night. And that was it. We couldn't make it, and I told Captain Buchanan on the *Endurance* that, by the following morning, we would be five miles away to the west of the island. There was no chance of getting across North-East Land. There was a great stretch of open water, and the ice was all broken up everywhere. So we would head, I said, straight for the ship, and it would take us possibly a week or more to get to or near the ship. Trying to get on to land might take us two weeks. What really depressed me most that night was the prospect that we might not make land at all, even Spitzbergen. But even if we didn't get to Spitzbergen, but got to the ship, then, by definition, we would have crossed the Arctic Ocean from one side to the other.

That night we didn't sleep too badly, in spite of everything. We slept out on our sledges, as usual. The following morning when we woke up we found to our surprise that Little Black-board Island was still there, in almost exactly the same spot. We had moved hardly more than a couple of hundred yards, and certainly not away from the island. We had moved, if anything, slightly closer to it. And so we set off straight away to have a look at it. I loaded up my cameras and took a ruck-sack.

The island was a little under a quarter of a mile away from the camp site itself, but from the edge of the ice floe on which we were situated it was about a hundred yards. The mush had widened since the previous day. A hundred yards – maybe a bit farther. It was moving all the time, vacillating and shifting, gyrating. Anyway, I loaded up all the cameras, two Nikons, a Rolleiflex and two movie cameras, and set off after Allan and Ken. It was a tricky operation. At that moment, the ice was quiet, but you could see just the slightest signs of movement. The whole thing was delicately poised; it was just held together by the floe pushing against the land, and was putting just sufficient pressure on the mush ice to hold it tight. Tight enough, that is, for a man to walk on it without its capsizing. It needed only to slacken off a couple of inches to loosen up to danger point. Fritz stayed on the edge of the floe, in case we needed the rubber dinghy. I went after Allan and Ken who spent some time trying to chop away some steps down a steep drop on to another pan of ice. I thought someone would have to keep an eye on this. From about the halfway point, I kept guard over the area. Meanwhile, they crept forward to see how far they could get. It was a reconnaissance trip just to see if a landing was feasible.

I kept walking backwards and forwards, checking the ice, and I was actually standing with Fritz when we saw Ken and Allan climb on to the land. We could just see two figures scrambling up the rocks. I immediately went after them, to see if I could get any pictures of the landing. The surprise had caught me unawares, and I had quite a distance to travel to catch them up. I moved forward as quickly as I could, but by the time I met up with them, they were halfway back already and the ice was treacherous. The risk of making a second trip to the island just to take some pictures seemed too big. Just as I was pondering over the decision, Fritz started yelling that the ice was beginning to move, so we all had to turn round and run for it. We had a scramble to get back on to the floe. The gyrating pans were all sloppy by that time. We got back on to the floe safely enough and then the whole area slackened off. We couldn't get across for the rest of the day. So that was it.

Thus we had no photographic record of the historic moment, but Allan and Ken had had the foresight, and the good sense, to bring back a couple of chunks of rock: a fairly small piece which Ken has, and a bigger piece about the size of a teacup which they brought back for me. It proved, as we had guessed, to be of granite. The critics, of course, will say that we carried it all the way across the Arctic Ocean! Perhaps the only answer is to send a geologist up to Little Blackboard Island to see if he can find a similar kind of granite.

There was no great rejoicing, then or at any other high points of the journey. In a way we were rather unemotional. Only two of us had made landfall, just as only Hillary and Tensing reached the summit of Everest. It's never quite the same if you

197

are represented in your feat by only a couple of members of the party. To get the full feeling of it, I think everyone has to get there simultaneously. In other words, it wasn't anything like the way I had dreamed it was going to be. I had visualized sledging up to land – literally sledging across pack ice which would bring us to landfast ice – and sledging across landfast ice right up to the tide crack – and then bumping across this tide crack on to land and stopping. It didn't work out that way. Instead, we found that only two of us got there and the ice wouldn't let us go back again.

We still had a long way to go to get to the ship, and we weren't really in a very safe position. At this point, the ship was about one hundred and forty miles to the south-west. It was far enough away, and the ice conditions were deteriorating quickly. Within the past four or five days, the ice had broken up all over the area – not just in one local area, to the north-east of Hinlopen Strait, but throughout the entire belt of ice which extended across to the north shores up to about fifteen miles away from the coast.

Had we been even a day later we might never have made landfall, and if we'd come a few days earlier, we might have made it without difficulty. We can never be sure either way. So we were not elated. We just had the satisfaction of knowing that two men representing the Expedition had made land. We 'had it in the bag'. No one can ever say we didn't complete the journey, though at the time there were so many other problems ahead, I couldn't relax and feel cheerful. I still felt I had the world on my shoulders.

The actual landing itself occurred at about 10.00 a.m. in the morning, or rather, 10.00 p.m. at night, since we were working twelve hours after phase, travelling at night-time and sleeping during the day. So it was 10.00 p.m., though to us it was effectively ten in the morning. The sun was at about the same altitude day and night as it went round and round the sky. I spent the rest of the day composing four messages. These all had to be carefully thought out and carefully coded, and Ken gave me a hand with this. While I was writing, he spent the time coding the previous message. By our evening – in fact, the following morning, the 29th – at about 6.30 a.m. on the morning of the 29th, the *Endurance* came up on the radio in their usual way saying 'Traction, Traction, this is warship *Endurance*.' I wanted Freddie to be the first to know that we had actually made land, but there was no way of letting him know short of sending a coded message which would take time to decode. I therefore had to send something that the *Endurance* wouldn't understand, but which Freddie would appreciate before I sent the rest in code. So the very first message I sent was for Freddie Church. He couldn't hear me from T-3, but he could hear *Endurance*. I just said, 'Freddie, cheers'. I remember the radio operator on the *Endurance* saying 'Well, that's all there is to the message.' And then he came back and asked, 'Well, is there any more?' and I said 'No, that's it.' He then said, 'Okay, I'll pass it on to Freddie, but I don't think he'll understand it.' He passed it on to Freddie, and Freddie said, 'Oh yes, I know what that means.'

I went straight on with the codes 19874, 69320 and so on for the other messages. There was one for the Chairman, Sir Miles Clifford, to pass on to the Queen, one direct to Prince Philip, the Patron, a general press release, and a short one to Captain Buchanan.

The text of the message to be passed on to Her Majesty was:

At 19.00 hrs GMT 29 May a landing was made on a small rocky island at Lat. 80°49′ N, Long. 20°23′ E after a journey of 3620 route miles from Point Barrow Alaska via the North Pole. I would be most grateful if you would inform H.M. The Queen that the first surface crossing of the Arctic Ocean has been accomplished, and accept for yourself and on behalf of your committee our warmest congratulations and thanks.

Crossing Party.

And for our Patron, I said:

We send our Patron warmest greetings from Lat. 80° 49′ N, Long. 20° 18′ E a point one mile west of a small rocky island on which today two of our party briefly set foot. With the crossing thus completed, and with H.M.S. *Endurance* only 100 miles to our south-west, it is tempting to relax, but this we dare not do for the ice all around us is badly broken and drifting rapidly towards the Greenland Sea. The next two weeks of sledging may well prove to be the most hazardous two weeks of the journey.

W. W. Herbert, Expdn. Ldr.

14 End of a Journey

ONCE WE HAD MADE LANDING, WE HEADED DIRECTLY FOR THE SHIP AS FAST AS WE POSSIBLY COULD, BUT THE WHOLE area was broken up by this time and was a chaos of ice. To the north-west there was a route which led on to what looked like a sizeable floe and we headed in that general direction. But once on the floe, we only had about two miles' travel before we got back into the rough stuff again. It was some of the roughest ice that we had come across since shortly after leaving winter quarters. Not only was it very broken up, it was constantly shifting about and jostling, and we were leaping from one floe or one pan of ice to another all the time. We had to keep close together or we might have got separated. Polar bears were also a menace; every day we were stalked by one or two. They seemed impossible to scare off. We just had to keep going in the hope that they would get bored and go away of their own accord, or, if they came too close, shoot them. Indeed, they were coming so thick and fast, we began to worry about our supplies of ammunition. With an accurate shot, it is possible to kill a polar bear with a ·270 high-velocity weapon, but this was generally beyond our powers of marksmanship. Bisley standards are impossible when you're out of breath and preoccupied with a team of excited dogs. So we always took three rifles to the polar bear and just let blast, trying to keep the number of bullets down to a minimum. It usually took two or three to make absolutely certain. We used the first one to drop the bear, the second one to make certain he wasn't going to get up quickly, and the third one, if necessary, just straight through the head at very close range. Though this seemed to be the surest way of doing it. We could not afford to spend three or four rounds per polar bear, so I sent a message to H.M.S. *Endurance* asking if they had any ·270 Winchester cartridges in their armoury, and, if not, could they stand by to drop us a rifle suitable for the job. We had about thirty rounds left by then which would only last for about ten polar bears – say, five days' supply. Without weapons, it would have been a risky business sledging along that coast. We even tried on one occasion throwing ice-axes at a bear, but it took no notice and came on. Once, Fritz threw one of my boots at a bear, which it promptly tore to pieces.

I wanted to sledge right up to the ship. Captain Buchanan knew this, and for his part was trying to get his ship as close to us as he could so that his helicopters could be of assistance. He was pushing his ship hard into the pack ice, north-eastwards, but was making only a mile or two a day at that time. I remember on the day that we made land, he came on the radio and said, 'Now look, you are within my range. I can get to you if there is an emergency, but you would have to leave everything behind – your sledges, your dogs, your records, everything.' It was a dilemma, for the ice had slowed down to about a mile a day. And then we were stopped altogether. For three days, we just drifted round and round in circles.

Another problem was that we were waiting for an airdrop. The Royal Canadian Air Force had very generously responded to a request from me for one airdrop more than we had originally scheduled. We needed this extra airdrop in order to give us a certain latitude. If, for instance, we found ourselves in a desperate position where we could not move the dogs across the water, but could move ourselves, our records and a minimum amount of gear, then we could have become a man-hauling party. This was obviously a thing we wouldn't do unless it became a question of saving our lives. So this final airdrop was partly to extend our period in the field by giving us extra food, and partly to drop the necessary equipment so that we could convert to a manhauling party, if necessary. In retrospect, I am sure we could have manhauled our equipment to the ship; but having come all the way across the Arctic Ocean with dogs, we wanted to get the dogs safely on to the ship also. In the event, we didn't take the manhauling gear with us; we just took the extra food. But waiting for the airdrop occupied a couple of days.

The airdrop itself went off perfectly in spite of poor weather conditions. After leaving us, the aircraft flew on directly to the *Endurance* and dropped the rest of the gear and extra dog food on a nearby floe. The *Endurance* then sent out helicopters and picked it up. It was the first thing that had happened to the crew of the *Endurance* in Spitzbergen waters which gave them any excitement, and it was the first contact, in a way, that they had had with the Expedition. It was also interesting that the R.C.A.F. reported that the ice we were in was the kind of ice the *Endurance* needed, and the ice they were in was exactly what we wanted. It was ironic that they should be stuck in good solid floes all around them while we were in an area which was completely broken up. It was, in fact, several days before we managed to extricate ourselves from this mess.

We had a debate over the next move. Because of his military training, Ken felt that the helicopter was an extended arm of the ship, and that if we were going to make for the ship, then all we had to do in effect was make for the point at which a helicopter could reach us. I could see the force of this as a logistic argument, but as a fitting finish to a polar journey with which I had now been involved for six years, I just could not take it. Fritz and Allan felt the same way as I did. We ought to make it to the ship if there was any chance. Fritz, in fact, had an even more ambitious plan which was to head straight for North-East Land and to climb right over the mountains, down the other side, cross the Hinlopen Strait south of the open water, and then do a complete climb over the Spitzbergen mountains down to Longyearbyen. This might have been possible, but it would have been a very long way round, and it would have meant that the *Endurance* couldn't possibly have waited for us. We would have had to come back by some other vessel, and as the *Endurance* had come north especially to pick us up, I felt the onus was on us to make an effort to reach them. In my original plan, I had estimated that we would make Longyearbyen by the 21st June, Midsummer's Day. To my embarrassment, the ship came up a month in advance of that date and was due to leave Spitzbergen waters on the 20th June.

My plan originally had been to sledge from north to south down the long fjord that penetrates deep into Spitzbergen, to climb over the mountains and down to Sassenfjord: there, I had imagined, sitting in Sassenfjord, mirrored in that tranquil pool of water, would be the *Endurance* waiting for us. We would come down off the ice cap and see the ship sitting in amongst the icebergs there. This was going to be the big moment of the whole journey. Unfortunately it was not possible, because the *Endurance* was not given permission to go within five miles of the coast; this meant they couldn't penetrate Ice Fjord and Sassenfjord and wait there for us to turn up. In an effort to be of some use to us, Captain Buchanan had therefore taken the ship up the north-west coast and then, keeping north of the five-mile limit, tried to penetrate the ice pack towards us.

For five or six days he pushed his ship into the pack ice in our direction until *Endurance* stuck solid. Admittedly, the weather was getting warmer and it was only a matter of time before the ice pack would loosen up. Nevertheless, taking a ship into solid pack ice was a calculated risk, and I felt myself under a special obligation to be co-operative. If they were making such efforts to get to us, then I had no right to go off in some other direction in order to fulfil a private ambition of making land and climbing over the mountains. Also, since Captain Buchanan had spent so long getting into the pack ice and getting thoroughly stuck, it was presumably going to take him almost as long to get out again.

There was every pressure on us to try and close the gap with the *Endurance*. At the point where we had made land, they could only pick up four men; if, on the other hand, we could close that gap to forty miles, they could take everything out – all the equipment, all the dogs, all the records. The target Captain Buchanan set was the maximum range of a helicopter when fully loaded, and I accepted it.

My romantic dream about how the journey should have ended had already been denied me. There was no time to make Spitzbergen, but at least I could make the ship. The ship was stuck. The ship was an island – no different in a sense from Spitzbergen. The vision I now had in mind was of four teams of dogs coming across the ice, approaching *Endurance* from the north. For the crew it would be a great spectacle. The whole drama of it appealed to me. It would be a fitting ending – the right kind of ending. It didn't have to be dramatic, but it had to be perfect. Somehow, if the end is a shambles, everything is spoiled.

So we kept pushing on, managing to make some progress, and suddenly we broke away from this area where we had been drifting around in circles. We made ten miles on one day and Peter Buchanan was delighted. I even started sending optimistic messages, 'We're going to be there in ten days' time, or five days, or four days, at this rate, and if you move three or four miles in our direction, we'll be there even quicker'. But things didn't work out. On the morning of the 10th June, I tuned up the radio. *Endurance* hadn't moved for about forty-eight hours. We were forty-two miles from the ship. Captain Buchanan's voice came over the air: 'I know how you feel about this, and I really would like you to come right up to the ship, but there's a lot of broken ice around here now and it looks very bad'. Not knowing fully our capabilities for travelling, he didn't want to be too definite; but he added that there was bad weather coming up, and in twenty-four hours a snowfall was forecast. The helicopters couldn't operate in a snowfall. However, he promised that he would wait for us.

He was very near his time limit. If it was going to take him as long to get out of the pack ice as it took to get in, then he should have left on the morning of the 9th and it was already the morning of the 10th. But he was prepared to wait another four days and risk getting back late in order to give us the chance of sledging right up to the ship. This seemed to me such a generous gesture that I felt obliged to make one in return. I acknowledged his message but then the radio conditions faded, and I had to go on to the Morse key. I tapped out a message saying in view of the weather situation and the possible snowfall within twenty-four hours, come and pick us up now. Fly the helicopters straight out. They were already airborne anyway. They just had to change their direction. It was a little while before the message was decoded. I think he was both pleased and a bit surprised, caught off guard perhaps, at this spontaneous capitulation to his wishes. Within two hours, the helicopters had landed and taken off the first load of gear.

As soon as it was confirmed that the two helicopters were on their way, I crawled out of the tent and gave the news to Allan, Fritz and Ken. The first load would be a cargo load, the second load would take Fritz and his dogs, and the other helicopter, his sledge. Each sortie would take one man and his dogs – the last person to go would be me. It all went so fast there was very little time to stop and think about anything. The helicopters were operating at the very limit of their range, and all they had on board was an observer and one photographer. The photographer stayed with us while the helicopters went back to the ship to offload the gear before coming out again. It was a mad rush. There was perhaps an hour to spare between the visits, but that hour was crammed with work, packing boxes, sorting things out into piles. We didn't have time to sit down and contemplate.

The huskies were put loose into the helicopter. They seemed quite happy, but the first couple of flights were awkward because we didn't know how many dogs we could put into each helicopter. The helicopters could only stay on the ground for a maximum of about five minutes. They couldn't switch the engines off for some reason I never fully understood. The temperature wasn't very low at that time, but presumably they felt safer if they kept the blades going. They were of course burning up fuel all the time, kicking up a wind and making a hell of a noise. Everything was panic and flap and bustle, and everyone was rushing around shouting 'Hurry up!'

I felt, I must admit, a little hostile towards the first man that greeted me. He wore a bone-dome helmet and a satanic beard, and his name I later discovered was 'Beest'. Later, on board ship, we were to become great friends, but on the ice he wanted me to rush. I didn't want to rush. I hadn't rushed for eighteen months, but his helicopter was sitting there, whirring away, kicking up an awful racket and blowing everything about. I found out later that they were so close to the maximum range at which they could operate with a heavy load that to have stayed an extra five or ten minutes on the ice could have been disastrous.

Dogs don't seem to mind being put in an aeroplane providing the engines are not running – but try putting dogs on a helicopter when the rotors are whizzing round and the whole machine is shaking! One has literally to wrestle them in and stand at the door fighting them back, until eventually, overcome by their fear, they cower on their bellies and start dribbling all over the floor.

Fritz, Allan and Ken were carried away and I was left with only a sledge, a tent and my team of dogs. I got busy packing up my gear, getting it ready to put in the helicopters, knowing they would want to be away in a hurry. When everything was ready, I sat on the sledge and had a smoke. It was a wonderful feeling being all by myself out there. For the first time in sixteen months I was further than five miles from the nearest man. This was something to be savoured. I just sat there and smoked, not thinking about anything in particular but just feeling good. I was neither sad about what I was leaving, nor excited about what I was going to. It was a sort of suspended state.

The helicopters came back, and the stillness and purity of the Arctic were shattered with noise and tainted with evil engine smells. So this was civilization. It hurt the ears. It was an intrusion. People were screaming at me, yelling, laughing, inviting me to parties. I had to rush. I had to lift dogs, push them into the helicopters. Lift sledges. Crawl in after the dogs and pacify them during the flight. Occasionally I took a glance out of the window – the ice below was really broken up, an absolute mess. I doubted very much if we could have got to the ship in less than ten days. I was going back to something I was unsure of. Everything was confused and happening too quickly. The helicopter banked and for a moment or two I could see the ship. It was framed in the window. It looked very small. I could see as we were coming in that the hangar on the flight deck was full of people.

We hovered over the deck for a second or two, then settled. The doors were flung open and the noise flooded in. Wind from the rotors was whipping the film of water on the flight deck, beating it slippery. I was pushing the dogs out of the helicopter door, and they were all scared. Their legs were kicking before they hit the deck and they took off as soon as their claws scratched the steel. There were sailors grabbing the dogs and disappearing with them, and I didn't bother. I knew that once the dogs were outside, someone was going to look after them, so I just hurled them out of the door and followed them. I jumped down on to the flight deck with a hell of a thud. Bloody hell, it was hard – the thud resonated all through the ship.

There was a great sea of faces directly ahead – a huge crowd of strangers, and so much wind from the rotors and noise from engines, I couldn't tell whether the sailors were shouting as I was swept in amongst them. Everyone seemed to be smiling – I could hear voices – and feel my hand being shaken. I was confused and too many emotions came crowding in at once. At that moment, I only knew that the journey was over.